D1575786

YOUR NEWBORN
BABY

YOUR NEWBORN BABY

EVERYTHING YOU NEED TO KNOW

BY MICHAEL KRAUSS
WITH SUE CASTLE

FEATURING JOAN LUNDEN

INTRODUCTION BY JEFFREY L. BROWN, M.D., F.A.A.P.

WARNER BOOKS

A Warner Communications Company

The advice in this book can be
a valuable addition to the advice
of your baby's doctor, and is designed
for your use under his or her care and direction.

Copyright © 1988 by Michael Krauss Productions, Inc.
Illustrations copyright © 1988 by Allan Neuwirth

All rights reserved.

Warner Books, Inc., 666 Fifth Avenue, New York, NY 10103

 A Warner Communications Company

Printed in the United States of America

First Printing: June 1988

10 9 8 7 6 5 4 3 2 1

Book Design by Nick Mazzella
Cover design by Don Puckey

Library of Congress Cataloging-in-Publication Data

Krauss, Michael, 1939–
   Your newborn baby.

   1. Infants (Newborn)—Care.   2. Infants—Care.
I. Castle, Sue.   II. Lunden, Joan.   III. Title.
[DNLM: 1. Infant Care—popular works.   2. Infant,
Newborn—popular works.   WS 113 K91y]
RJ253.K73   1988   649'.122   87-29563
ISBN 0-446-51374-1

To my wife,
my mother and my father . . . three of
the best parents on the face of this earth.
I love them all very much!

CONTENTS

INTRODUCTION:
YOUR NEWBORN BABY: EVERYTHING YOU NEED TO KNOW

JEFFREY L. BROWN, M.D., F.A.A.P.

IN HIS INTRODUCTION TO this book, Michael Krauss relates some of the emotions he felt as a new parent. His feelings are very similar to those which are experienced by most parents after bringing home their new babies. There are few life experiences that are more exciting, create more happiness or can produce more stress. This is a time when parents become related by a common relative for the first time and develop an extra sense of closeness by sharing a common goal. The magical quality felt while watching your own baby breathing, moving its fingers and toes, and sucking at the nipple is difficult to match. However, bright, organized and otherwise competent people sometimes become befuddled, sensitive, clumsy and irrational as soon as they leave the protective environment of the hospital. Their desire to do everything "the right way" may interfere with their ability to enjoy the baby to the fullest. After all, keeping the baby fed, healthy and happy is a very major responsibility.

Instructional materials such as books, tapes, magazine articles and television programs have all become an important source of information for today's modern parents. There has never been a time when more expert advice has been available about medicine, psychology and child raising than during the past few years. And it couldn't have come at a better time. Now that many mothers are working outside the home and extended family members are less accessible to a more mobile population, child-care teaching aids have become a great help to parents who might otherwise have been left out on a limb.

Professional groups such as the American Academy of Pediatrics and independent, responsible individuals like Joan Lunden, Michael Krauss and his excellent staff of writers (most especially Sue Castle) have used very creative methods for keeping parents properly informed about the newer and older ways of keeping our children healthy, emotionally and physically. As a practicing pediatrician, working with them on the home-videocassette edition of *Your Newborn Baby: Everything You Need to Know*, and their child-care shows, *Mother's Day* and *Mothers' Minutes*, has been very exciting for me because they have been very effective at reducing much of the anxiety that new parents feel about coping with the daily problems associated with child raising.

In addition to the flood of useful information from ''professional'' experts, parents continue to be confronted with advice from the traditional ''amateur'' experts. Relatives, friends and even strangers all offer opinions and give advice whether it is asked for or not. Not surprisingly, much of this advice is contradictory, and everyone who gives it seems *so* secure while telling novice parents what to do. It is unfortunate that this barrage of information sometimes makes new parents forget just how important and reliable common sense and intuition can be. Insecure parents may then become too afraid to make decisions on their own and rely almost entirely on the opinions of others. Although looking for advice is reassuring and helpful for problem solving, it is a terrible mistake when mothers and fathers give up their role as parents and allocate it to strangers who cannot do nearly as well as they can.

As a parent, you will find that the material covered in this book is extremely well-organized and thought out. It should be used as a guide as you are entering into unfamiliar territory. It will help to familiarize you with diapers, baby baths, breastfeeding, bottles and all of the day-to-day activities that are involved in infant care. The information presented here reflects the thinking of pediatricians and other child-care experts that works best for the great majority of parents and babies. However, each baby-parent combination is different, and the solutions to problems that work well in one household may not work well in another. For that reason, this book, and others offering medical and parenting advice, should be thought of as containing many helpful hints, but not strict rules. When parents refuse to pay attention to their own common sense and intuition they are the most likely to go astray. If advice is received by you as a parent and seems to be right, it usually is. But, when it seems wrong, if it doesn't make sense, or if it doesn't match up with your household routines and your personal priorities, you should carefully reevaluate it before accepting it.

Enjoy this excellent baby care book as an introduction into the world of babies and parenting. Then strike out on your own as a parent. Be your own person. Most importantly, don't be afraid to trust your own feelings, beliefs and intuition as you make the decisions necessary to keep your child happy and healthy.

YOUR NEWBORN
BABY

CONCEPTION

IT SEEMS LIKE ONLY yesterday that Joan and I were expecting our first child—but now Jamie is already seven, Lindsay is four and our third beautiful daughter, Sarah, has just arrived! Boy (pardon the expression), I still remember so clearly how we felt as that **first** due date drew nearer. Like so many other first-time parents, we were happy and excited, just counting the days. But we were also anxious at the thought of all that responsibility. Would we actually know how to take care of a newborn baby? Although, if you stop to think about it, all those questions and doubts are really normal. After all, until now Joan and I had always been a daughter and a son. Suddenly we were going to be a mother and a father . . . and parents are supposed to know everything, right? But how?

Well, we soon learned that in the first place, newborns may be the most helpless of any species, but they aren't made of glass or else the human race wouldn't have been around for so long. And another thing, while you may not have had any experience being a parent, your baby doesn't know that and you'll both learn from each other. Just remember, **you don't have to be perfect!**

Of course, the best way to help relieve some of that anxiety is to get answers to as many questions as possible. In that respect, Joan and I were lucky—in the world of TV talk shows, it's easy to go straight to the experts in every field! I became incredibly involved, first in Joan's pregnancy, and then in the anxious but exuberant experience of being a new father!

That's when I realized there were millions of other parents like Joan and me who wanted and needed information that was visual, practical and, most important, was conveyed with what I call a ''sense of human'' . . . and a sense of humor! But as of yet, there wasn't one television show dedicated solely to the subject of parenting. Fortunately, I had just started my own production company,

1

so our first project became *Mother's Day*, the ACE award-winning half-hour show featuring celebrity parents and experts from every field. Our next parenting project was MOTHERS' MINUTES on ABC-TV in which Joan shares our personal experiences as parents and the advice we've gotten from hundreds of experts.

Finally, we had the opportunity to make the home video, *Your Newborn Baby, Everything You Need To Know*—the very idea that had first started me in the direction of producing parenting shows. In a sense this was **my** way of "giving birth" to something I felt was worthwhile. By this time our second daughter, Lindsay, had arrived and we had a pretty good feel for the kinds of questions that come up . . . especially at two A.M.! But of course we went through extensive research in the course of producing this tape.

Our own pediatrician, Dr. Jeffrey Brown, who's written several excellent books on infant care, was both our behind-the-scene and on-tape consultant. A nursing mother from the La Leche League came on to demonstrate the best way to breastfeed a baby. And the American Academy of Pediatrics was not only called daily during preparation of the script, but they also sent a doctor to the set so we could be sure that everything we shot followed the Academy's guidelines. The result was very satisfying. We got tons of great reviews and *TV Guide* praised it as "a superior infant-care tape, also one of the best instructional home-video programs ever produced!"

Now, for those parents who don't own a VCR or would like a supplement to the tape, we've created this book. It covers all the same areas—from "Choosing Your Baby's Doctor" to "Your Baby's Sleep," but since it doesn't have to fit within the restraints of a one-hour tape, we can go into each area in even more detail. While it isn't everything that you will ever know about babies, or everything that exists to know, I believe this book contains everything that doctors feel you NEED to know to take good care of your newborn baby. I hope this information goes a long way toward helping you relieve your anxiety. There's nothing like those first few weeks with your baby . . . so relax and enjoy every minute! It all goes by so quickly!

CHAPTER 1
CHOOSING YOUR BABY'S DOCTOR

ONE OF THE MOST important things you should do in preparing for your newborn's arrival is to choose the doctor who will be caring for your baby. Why is it best to decide on a doctor ahead of time? Well, in the first place, he or she will be able to help you in making some other decisions such as whether or not to breastfeed, or, if you have a boy, whether to have him circumcised.

JOAN: Our pediatrician, Dr. Jeffrey Brown, like many other doctors, also gives out printed information with his specific recommendations on newborn care. We had time to become familiar with his advice and that relieved a lot of anxiety. Many expectant parents spend months becoming experts on every aspect of pregnancy and delivery, and then are suddenly panicked by a whole new set of questions when their baby arrives!

Another reason to choose your baby's doctor before delivery is that you'll have the time to find a doctor who you trust and respect, but just as important, a doctor who listens to you and respects your ability as parents. So how do you find someone who fits the bill?

GETTING RECOMMENDATIONS

First, you begin your search by getting the names and addresses of pediatricians or "family practice" doctors in your area. Remember that the location of your doctor's office is important. It should be fairly close to your home, not only in case of emergencies, but also because visits to the doctor have an uncanny way of coinciding with heavy rains or snows! Here are some good sources for recommendations:

- Your obstetrician
- Nurses who work in the emergency room or pediatric unit of your local hospital
- The pediatric department of a nearby medical school
- You can also ask friends who share your views on parenting—but keep in mind that a lay person may NOT be the best judge of a doctor's ability.

If some names turn up more than once, it's a good indication that you're on the right track!

JOAN: When we moved to an unfamiliar area, I began my search for a pediatrician by talking to our real estate agent who's a member of the local Chamber of

Commerce, several mothers I knew in the area and the woman who runs a highly recommended nursery school. I asked two basic questions: "What DO you like about your doctor?" and "What DON'T you like about him (or her)?"

Joan and I also prefer a group practice which we feel has lots of advantages. One is that our children's records are readily available to the covering doctor when Dr. Brown is not on call. Also, it's reassuring to our girls that they never have to go to an unfamiliar office or doctor. Another bonus: one of the doctors in the practice is a woman and a great role model for the girls.

GETTING INFORMATION

The next step is to pick out two or three doctors and call their offices, but it's best to avoid calling on Monday morning since that's usually the busiest time. You should explain to the receptionist that you're expecting a baby, Dr. So-and-So has been highly recommended and you'd like some information about the office procedures.

You should be able to tell a lot about the tone of the office by the willingness of the receptionist or nurse to answer your questions. But if it's a busy time, don't be put out if you're asked to call back later. (If you have a friend who is using this doctor, she may also be able to give you some of the basic answers.) Here are the important things to find out:

- What are the regular office hours? (For working mothers, evening or Saturday hours can be a real bonus.)
- What is the usual fee schedule? (Doctors in the same area generally have comparable fees.)
- Does the doctor have a specific telephone calling hour for non-urgent problems and is there a charge for these calls? (It's especially important for new parents to feel they can call about anything that worries them.)
- Will the doctor accept your insurance and who is responsible for sending forms to the company?
- How often are well-baby check-ups recommended? Are

these scheduled during special hours or is there a special waiting room so your baby won't be exposed to sick children who are also waiting to see the doctor?

- How far in advance do you have to schedule appointments?
- How much time is allowed for appointments?

Once you're satisfied with the office procedures, the final question should be "Can I schedule an appointment to meet with the doctor?" If the answer is "He's too busy" or "She doesn't feel that's necessary," move on to the next doctor on your list. Fortunately, most doctors are happy to meet with prospective parents, and even if there's a charge for the visit, it's worth it.

GETTING TO KNOW THE DOCTOR

Many parents meet their baby's doctor for the first time at the hospital or at the first check-up and realize they don't really like him or her. Yet, by this time, they may be reluctant to change. So it's important to interview the doctor ahead of time to make sure you feel comfortable with him or her and that you're on the same wave length.

JOAN: **It may have had something to do with my father being a doctor, although other people have admitted the same feeling, but I viewed doctors as being omnipotent, even god-like. So the idea of interviewing a doctor to find out if HE was good enough for ME was difficult and a little embarrassing! But I had changed obstetricians twice before I found someone who made me feel confident and comfortable, so I knew this was an important part of choosing a doctor for our children.**

Michael and I met with several doctors before Jamie was born and I wondered how they felt about being interviewed. Dr. Jeffrey Brown, who became our daughter's pediatrician, reassured me that most doctors don't mind. He also pointed out that "It's very important to know if a doctor does mind, because it

means that he may not be available to you at other times when it's even more important.''

When you go for the interview, you can learn a lot even before you see the doctor. The waiting room should be designed to make children feel comfortable, with small chairs and plenty of toys and books. And if there seems to be a back-up of waiting parents, you should ask if this is usually the case. Remember, your time is valuable, too.

Then, when you meet with the doctor, be ready with your questions. In fact, have them written down, so you can get the most out of your visit. Here are some things to find out:

- How do I get in touch with you in case of an emergency?
- Who covers for you if you aren't available and how do I reach that doctor?
- Do you mind being called even if it turns out to be a minor problem?
- Now, if you have strong feelings about anything, such as breastfeeding, schedules or medication, ask the doctor's views. Remember, you want someone who will support you, not fight you or intimidate you.

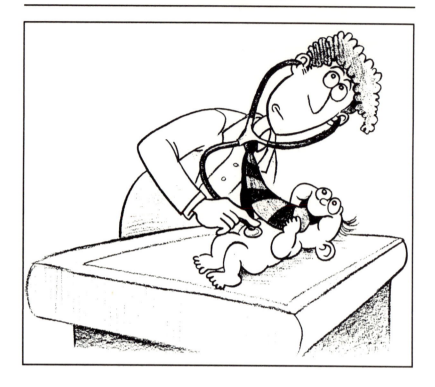

Finally, the most important questions are ones that parents have to ask themselves, "Does the doctor really listen to my concerns?" "Does the doctor respect my opinions?" If the answers are "Yes," then you know you've chosen the right doctor for your baby.

> JOAN: **Dr. Brown has certainly answered all our questions over the years, but it took a couple years before I got up the nerve to ask him why he and lots of other pediatricians always wear a bow tie. His answer should have been obvious, "Because the babies like to eat the long ones!"**

CHAPTER 2
DECISIONS BEFORE YOUR BABY IS BORN

ONCE YOU'VE CHOSEN YOUR baby's doctor, there are some other decisions that you should make well in advance of your delivery date—babies often arrive ahead of schedule! And you now have the advantage of being able to discuss these issues with the doctor who will be caring for your baby!

BREAST OR BOTTLE?

One of the most important decisions you must make before going to the hospital is whether or not you are going to breastfeed your baby. Because if you aren't, you'll be given medication soon after delivery to keep your milk from coming in. But if you are planning to breastfeed, you should start as soon as possible after delivery, even in the delivery room. Your baby's sucking will encourage your milk to come in.

> JOAN: **Also, if you decide a few months ahead of time to nurse your baby, you'll have a chance to toughen up your nipples and that can help prevent soreness. Whenever you have the opportunity, leave your breasts exposed to air, friction and sun—just be careful not to get them sunburned! It's best to wash your nipples only with plain water, since soap can cause them to dry and crack. Then, after your bath or shower, you should rub your nipples gently with a towel. In the last few weeks, it's a good idea to wear your nursing bra and leave the flaps down part of the day.**

As to the question of whether you should breastfeed your baby, the answer is unequivocally "Yes!" Many experts, including the American Academy of Pediatrics and the U.S. Surgeon General, strongly recommend breast milk as "the ideal food for infants during the first year of life." And that shouldn't be surprising. Breast milk was the main, often the only, source of nutrients since the beginning of the human race! If a mother couldn't nurse, her baby was fed by a wet nurse.

Then, at the beginning of this century, cow's milk modified with sugar and water was developed as a substitute for breast milk. When commercial formulas became readily available, their convenience led to an increase in bottle feeding, especially among middle- and upper-class mothers who viewed this as a sign of progress. Gradually, breastfeeding became thought of as unnecessary, even socially undesirable. By 1955 only eighteen percent of infants born in this country were being breastfed.

The tide turned when studies began to show there were definite advantages to breast milk over formulas, and doctors started encouraging mothers to breastfeed their babies. By 1971, twenty-five percent of infants were being breastfed and the figure increased to fifty-eight percent by 1981. Today it's still rising.

> JOAN: **When I decided to breastfeed Jamie, who was born in 1980, many people asked me "Why would you want to do that?" especially since I planned to go back to work. I really had to explain my reasons for wanting to nurse. Now, seven years later, everyone accepts this as the usual way to feed a newborn.**

What are the advantages of breastfeeding that have convinced so many doctors and parents?

- Most important, human breast milk is designed by nature to supply specific nutrients in the amounts that are best for human infants. Cow's milk, which is the basis of most formulas, may be fine for baby calves but it doesn't have the same composition as human milk.
- Breast milk contains a higher level of cholesterol than formulas, and for infants, this is beneficial. Cholesterol is essential in the synthesis of bile acids which are necessary for the absorption of fat. It may also be important in the development of mechanisms to handle the processing of dietary cholesterol later in life.
- Breast milk is more easily digested than formula and that means less chance of spitting up.
- Infants are rarely allergic to breast milk, and those who are breastfed for at least two months may be less likely to develop food allergies later. This is an important consideration if food allergies seem to "run" in the family.
- Breastfed infants are also less likely to develop infections, especially respiratory and intestinal ones. Breast milk gives your baby immunity to specific bacteria such as E. coli and staphylococcus, and may protect him against some fungus infections and viruses.
- A new study at the Johns Hopkins School of Public Health indicates that breastfeeding may contribute to straighter teeth. Nursing infants use their tongues differently and suck more vigorously with their mouth muscles which contributes to proper alignment of the jawbone.

JOAN: **And as if all these advantages aren't enough, breast milk is the most economical way to feed your baby. This is one time you can get the best without paying more for it! It's also the most convenient way —there's always a ready supply and the milk's always the same temperature. I certainly appreciated that at two A.M.! Breastfeeding also gives me a private time when I can't do anything but just sit and relax. I believe this really helps bonding with your baby.**

If you still have reservations about whether you want to breast-feed your baby or if you have doubts about your ability to breastfeed, talk it over with your baby's doctor and some mothers who are doing it. There are lots of places you can get support, and a little later, in Chapter 6, you'll learn everything you need to know about breastfeeding your baby. So why not at least give it a try. You can always switch to formula, but you can't go back the other way. Of course, if you do decide not to breastfeed, don't feel guilty. Commercial infant formulas are designed to provide adequate nutrition.

SUGAR WATER

JOAN: **In some hospital nurseries, nursing babies are routinely given bottles of sugar water. When Jamie was brought to my room to nurse, there would also be a little bottle of sugar water tucked in the bassinet. I felt it was sort of a hint to me that I might not have enough milk to satisfy her, but our pediatrician re-assured me that newborns really don't need sugar water or even plain water.**

In fact, bottles of sugar water are not only unnecessary, but they can also interfere with establishing successful breastfeeding. If your baby isn't very hungry, he may not nurse as long and it's the nursing that stimulates your milk production. Also, the nipple on the bottle can be very confusing to a baby who's just trying to get the hang of nursing from his mother's nipple.

So, if you're planning to breastfeed, check on whether the

hospital nursery pushes sugar water. If they do, ask your baby's doctor to put in a tactful word that the bottles shouldn't be given.

> JOAN: **But your doctor isn't always around. I think a lot of women are intimidated by hospital nurses. I mean, here are all these women who have gone to school to learn all about babies! Even so, I've learned that if you see something being done with the baby you don't like, you shouldn't be afraid to tell the nurse. After all, it's YOUR baby!**

PREVENTING EYE INFECTIONS

For years, silver nitrate drops were routinely put in a baby's eyes within a short time after birth. This treatment helps prevent serious infections that might have been passed from the mother to the baby's eyes during the trip through the birth canal. Left untreated, these infections could lead to blindness. However, there are some drawbacks to the use of silver nitrate. It is not effective against the chlamydia organism, a common cause of newborn eye infections. It is also very irritating to the eye, making the baby fussy and unable to see clearly.

Fortunately, there are alternatives to silver nitrate. The American Academy of Pediatrics and The National Society to Prevent Blindness have approved the use of the antibiotics erythromycin and tetracycline, either in the form of drops or ointment. These antibiotics do prevent chlamydial infections and they are less irritating to the newborn's eyes.

You should check with the hospital to see which treatment is routinely used. If silver nitrate is still being given, discuss the alternative use of erythromycin or tetracycline with your doctor and your baby's doctor. Then, be sure the necessary arrangements are made with the hospital well before it's time for your baby's first look at the world.

> JOAN: **Our new baby, Sarah, was given erythromycin which is the hospital's standard procedure.**

CIRCUMCISION

Another procedure that became routine in the United States, although uncommon in the rest of the world, is the circumcision of male babies. By 1970, eighty-five percent of all babies born in this country were circumcised. Circumcision is an operation which cuts the foreskin away from the glans, or rounded end of the penis.

Why is this done? Well, for centuries, circumcision has been an important part of Jewish religious law. However, in the late 1800's, it became favored among non-Jews because it was thought to be a deterrent to masturbation. After this was shown to be an old wives' tale, circumcision still gained support because it was considered more hygenic. There was also the theory that circumcised males were less susceptible to penile cancer and their sexual partners were less likely to develop cervical cancer.

All these reasons, except for religious ones, have been strongly disproven. There is no evidence that circumcision helps prevent cancer or venereal disease. As for the argument that an uncircumcised penis is difficult to keep clean, the Academy says the best advice during early childhood is to "Leave it alone." Don't try to retract the foreskin to clean underneath. After the foreskin has fully separated from the glans and is easily retracted, usually by the age of five, the area only requires the same washing as any other body part.

In 1975, the American Academy of Pediatrics issued a statement that "there is no absolute medical indication for routine circumcision of the newborn." The American College of Obstetricians and Gynecologists also supports this conclusion. Actually, the only medical reason for circumcising newborns is the very rare condition where a malformed foreskin completely closes the penile opening and prevents the baby from passing urine.

Even though there are no medical benefits from routine circumcision, many people might think, "Well, it couldn't hurt." The sad fact is that the procedure is painful since it is usually done without any anesthetic. And, as with any surgery, there is the possibility of bleeding and infection, especially since the area is then enclosed in a diaper. The Academy also points out that the foreskin is meant by nature to shield the sensitive glans from being irritated by urine and feces. Once this protection is lost, the glans and the urinary opening may become irritated, infected or even ulcerated.

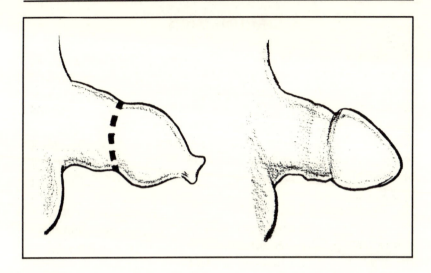

So, if there are no medical advantages and some potential disadvantages, why are a majority (fifty-nine percent in 1985) of male babies born in the United States still being circumcised every year? Aside from religious circumcision, which is not at issue, many parents agree to have it done because they are under the vague impression that it is necessary. Other parents want their child to look like the other little boys, or like the father if he is circumcised.

Of course, parents should make the decision they feel most comfortable with, but it should be an informed decision. Before your baby's arrival, discuss the procedure with your obstetrician and your pediatrician. You can also contact the American Academy of Pediatrics for more information.

If you decide to have your baby circumcised, their recommendation is to wait at least 12 to 24 hours after birth. By then the baby's vital signs have stabilized and any conditions that could cause complications have been identified. The procedure should be done only by a well-trained physician, usually your obstetrician or pediatrician. Religious circumcision is traditionally performed eight days after birth, by a trained and certified layman called a mohel (pronounced moy'-el). You might also discuss with your doctor the possibility of using a local anesthetic. A study has shown that it reduces crying and other signs of stress without harming the baby.

Remember, make your decision about circumcision well before your delivery date, and make it an informed decision.

ROOMING-IN

Another decision you should make before going to the hospital—actually it could play a part in choosing the hospital—is whether or not you want your baby to "room-in" with you. Many mothers prefer having their babies with them as much as possible, instead of having the baby sleep in the nursery and brought in for feedings. One advantage is that by the time you go home, you've really become self-confident in caring for your baby. It can also help establish breastfeeding since your baby can nurse as soon as he's hungry.

On the down side, you probably won't be getting as much rest if your baby is with you all the time and you may need that rest if you're feeling exhausted after the delivery. What's important is to check into the options that are offered by your hospital. If you want rooming-in, find out exactly how much time your baby really will be able to spend with you. Some hospitals won't allow babies to stay with their mothers during visiting hours or at night. Also ask whether a private room is required for rooming-in.

JOAN: **When I was in the hospital with my first baby, I was determined to have her with me all the time, even though I was warned this would be tiring. It only took a day or so to realize there was no way I was going to be able to get enough sleep. Every time she sputtered or cried—newborns aren't quiet sleepers— I would get up to check on her . . . then I couldn't get back to sleep! So, with my doctor's reassurance not to feel guilty, I worked out a system of partial rooming-in where I sent her to the nursery for short periods of time. But I made the nurses promise not to give her any bottles and to bring her back to me as soon as she was hungry. This demand feeding is so important when you're breastfeeding.**

I used this system again with Lindsay and our new baby, Sarah, and it's been a good compromise!

SMOKING

JOAN: **If you smoke, there's another decision you should make before your baby is born—TO STOP SMOKING! As a board member of the American Lung Association, I strongly support their position that smoking is dangerous to unborn babies. Many studies have shown if a woman smokes during pregnancy, her baby's birth weight and growth during the first year is reduced. Some of the other indisputable effects range from depressed breathing movements during fetal life, to cancer, respiratory disorders and heart disease in later years.**

The American Academy of Pediatrics also recommends—DON'T SMOKE WHEN PREGNANT! They further warn about the effects of passive smoking after the baby is born, "Children of parents who smoke have more respiratory infections, bronchitis, pneumonia and reduced pulmonary function than children of non-smokers." So the message is clear—if you're pregnant and you smoke, MAKE THE DECISION TODAY TO STOP!

CHAPTER 3
PREPARING THE NEST

JUST AS BIRDS MAKE a cozy nest for their offspring, it's a natural instinct to prepare a nursery for your baby, even if you only have a little space in the corner of a room. It's also a lot easier if you get the basics ready before your baby's arrival.

> JOAN: **I'm the kind of person who really likes to feel I'm organized and prepared, especially since I try to work right up until my delivery date. So the nesting instinct hits me hard around the eighth month when I realize there are only eight weeks to go!**

Nowadays the problem is there's so much in the way of equipment and clothing that it's a tough job deciding on what your baby really needs. Well, in this chapter, you'll learn about choosing basic items that are practical and safe so your baby will have a cozy nest!

YOUR BABY'S CRIB

Your baby is going to spend a lot of time in his crib, and it can be one of the safest places for him or one of the most dangerous! The shocking statistics from the U.S. Consumer Product Safety Commission show that more infants die every year in accidents involving cribs than with any other product intended for children. Thousands of other infants are injured seriously enough to require treatment in hospital emergency rooms.

What Makes A Crib Unsafe?

1. A decorative cut-out that may entrap a baby's head.
2. A missing crib slat, or more than two and three-eighth inches between the slats, may also result in entrapment and strangulation.
3. Corner posts that extend more than five-eighths of an inch may get caught in the baby's clothing if the baby stands up.
4. Sides that aren't high enough to discourage an older baby from trying to climb out.
5. If you can fit more than two fingers between the mattress and the side of the crib, the mattress is too small. An infant can suffocate if his head or body becomes wedged between the mattress and the side of the crib.
6. A thin plastic covering, like a trash bag, on the mattress. The plastic film may cling to a child's face and cause suffocation. A pillow should not be in a crib. (See page 20.)

As you can see, all these hazards can be eliminated. In 1974, the Consumer Product Safety Commission issued regulations for all new cribs made in America that require:

*   the space between slats or spindles to be two and three-eighth inches or less.

- the sides of the crib (in raised position) to be twenty-six inches above the mattress bottom, and (in lowered position) to be at least nine inches above the top of the mattress.
- the dropside latches be safe from accidental release by a baby inside the crib.
- the crib mattress to fit snugly.

Using A Secondhand Crib

Now, if you're using an older crib, or you buy a secondhand crib and you're not sure of the year it was made, be sure to check and see that the crib conforms to the regulations. But what if it doesn't?

- If the crib has corner posts, either unscrew them or saw them off flush with the headboard or footboard.
- If the slats are more than two and three-eighth inches apart, and you have no other choice, you must use bumper pads that fit around the inside of the entire crib. Make sure the

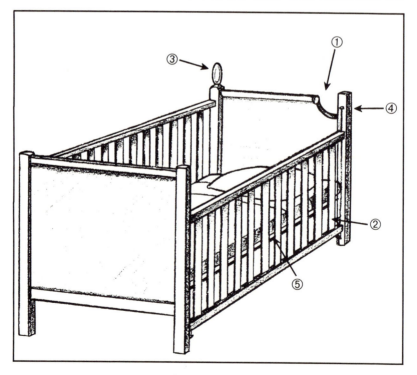

bumpers are securely tied, on the outside of the crib, in at least six places and trim off any extra length on the ties. Again, this type of crib is not recommended.

- If the mattress does not fit snugly (you can fit more than two fingers between the mattress and the side of the crib), replace the mattress. If you can't, and you must use the crib, roll up large towels and place them between the mattress and the crib sides.

- Finally, a word of warning about the finish on older cribs. In 1978, a regulation went into effect that limited the amount of lead in paints (lead is dangerous if it is ingested). Since babies love to chew on cribs, play it safe and refinish the crib with a high-quality household enamel paint that is labeled safe for use on children's products. The same also goes for varnishes and wood stains. If you're not sure of a product, check with the U.S. Consumer Product Safety Commission. After refinishing, let the paint dry thoroughly so there are no fumes that can irritate your baby.

It might also be a good idea to write to the crib's manufacturer, giving the model number, to check whether there were any problems with the crib. Some of the more reputable companies will make this information available and even have replacement kits for parts that proved hazardous.

Some Safety Tips

Whether your baby's crib is old or new, it's important to use it properly. And remember, your little newborn is going to grow quickly!

- If you use bumper pads, make sure they fit around the entire crib and can be tied or snapped to the crib in at least six places. Ties should always be fastened on the outside of the crib where the baby can't reach them, and any excess length should be cut off.
  (Note: When your baby is able to stand up in the crib, get rid of the bumpers. They make an easy foothold for trying to climb out!)

- Periodically check and tighten the screws and bolts that hold the crib together.
- If the mattress is supported by hangers, check to see they are secured whenever you have moved the crib or turned the mattress.
- Make sure you don't place the crib near any cords, like a drapery pull, that your baby can reach.
- Never hang any stringed object, such as a toy on a string or a laundry bag, on the crib post or anywhere a child could become caught in it and strangle. Cut off any strings or loops on toys you place in the crib.
- Crib gyms and other toys that are suspended across the crib should be installed securely so they can't fall into the crib. When your baby is able to push himself up on his hands and knees, remove the gym so he can't pull it down or become entangled.
- You must also be careful not to hang anything on a wall next to the crib. We made that mistake! When Jamie was a baby, we hung up a wonderful gift from the Disney people . . . a picture of Minnie Mouse that said ''Congratulations on your new baby!'' One day it fell and landed right in the crib. Fortunately Jamie wasn't in it!

- As soon as your baby can pull himself up, adjust the mattress to its lowest position and always lock the side rail to its highest position.
- Finally, don't put a pillow, even a decorative one, in the crib. Your baby will find it easier to breathe if her head rests on a firm, flat mattress. And if a newborn's head gets trapped under a large pillow, there could be some risk of suffocation. The same goes for that big stuffed animal that's so cute. Wait until your baby is able to push it out of the way.

JOAN: **Besides, as Dr. Brown points out, that darling teddy can soon become a dust bag shaped like a bear . . . not a great thing to sleep with if allergies run in the family!**

A BASSINET OR CRADLE

If you don't have room for a crib or you haven't yet chosen one, don't worry. Your little newborn doesn't even need a crib for the first couple of months. A bassinet or cradle will do just fine.

JOAN: **For our babies, we often use a basket with handles. It's so handy for visiting, going to a restaurant and when I bring the baby to my office. But we are always careful to only put it down where it can't fall. Actually the floor is the safest place! Now there are bassinet stands available and I've found they're really convenient. It also saves your back!**

Actually, it's not a bad idea to try to borrow a bassinet or cradle since you won't be using it for too long. But whether you buy or borrow, make sure it's well-built. A baby can be injured if the bottom breaks, or if it tips over or collapses.

- Look for one that has a sturdy bottom and a wide, stable base.
- Periodically, check the screws and bolts to see if they are tight.

- If the legs fold for storage, there must be secure locks that prevent the legs from folding while in use.
- Follow the manufacturer's recommendations on the appropriate weight and size of babies who can safely use the bassinet or cradle. When it's time, make the move to a crib.

A CHANGING TABLE

JOAN: **Of course, any flat surface like a table or dresser can be made into a changing table by adding a soft pad. But let's face it—you're going to be changing diapers many times a day for at least two years . . . if you're lucky! It will be so much easier on your back if you get a regular changing table that's at a comfortable height. I also remember when we first went shopping for nursery furniture and the salesman recommended a large table. My first thought was "It's so big and it will take up so much room." But am I**

**glad I listened and put practicality above aesthetics!
At work I had a small changing table, because that's
all there was room for, and I really learned to appre-
ciate the big one at home. You'll soon have to cope
with a squirming baby who knows how to turn over
. . . so think ahead!**

There's also the question of safety. Each year, an estimated
1,400 babies will require emergency room treatment for injuries
related to changing tables, the majority of them caused by falls!
Remember, it only takes a second for a baby to roll over and fall.
Even if she hasn't yet discovered how, there's always that first time.
Joan and I learned the hard way when Jamie was a baby. She rolled
off our bed, right in front of our eyes, and cut her lip. Boy, was
there a lot of blood and did we panic! When we rushed her to the
hospital's emergency room, the doctor said we were in worse shape
than Jamie. Fortunately it was only a little cut, but it was a big
lesson!

So here are some safety rules to follow:

- Look for a table that has safety straps and ALWAYS USE
  THEM!
- Even with the straps, you should NEVER leave your baby.
- Make sure all the supplies you need are kept within your
  reach, but out of your baby's. Look for a table that has
  handy shelves or side pockets. You can even hang a shoe
  bag on the side.

A BATH TUB

You can always bathe your baby in the kitchen sink. Just put
a folded towel or spongy pad under her so she's more comfortable
and won't slip. However, you could also use a plastic baby tub,
one with a foam insert will help your baby to feel more secure, or
a soft inflatable tub. These tubs are inexpensive and you can bathe
your baby anywhere that's comfortable and convenient for you.

Later on, in Chapter 9, you'll learn everything you need to
know about making bathtime a safe and enjoyable time.

AN INFANT SEAT

A reclining seat is a nice change for your baby who might get a little bored always being on his back or tummy. It's also convenient for carrying him around the house and for feeding. The seats are intended for use from birth to about five months, but when your baby is little, he will probably end up slumped in a corner. You can help him sit a little straighter by placing a rolled-up towel or blanket between him and the sides of the seat.

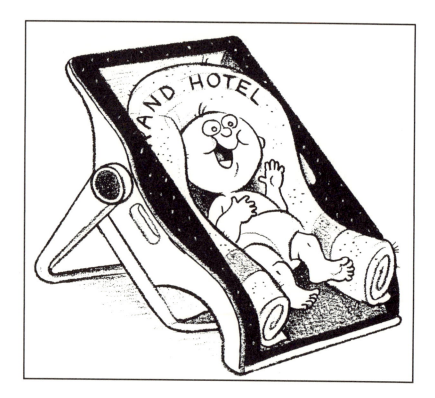

Some Safety Tips

An infant seat is really convenient, but it can also be dangerous if it's not used properly. The Consumer Product Safety Commission estimates 3,700 children each year are injured seriously enough in accidents associated with these seats to require emergency room treatment. Most of these injuries result from infants falling out of the seats, or the entire seat falling while the infant is sitting in it. Keep in mind that an active infant can move or tip a seat by pushing off on other objects with her feet. So, when buying or using an infant seat:

- Look for one with a wide, sturdy base for stability.
- Make sure there is a safety belt and always use it! This helps to keep your baby from arching his back and throwing himself out of the seat.
- If the seat does not already have non-skid feet, attach rough surfaced adhesive strips to the underside.
- If the seat uses wire-supporting devices which snap on the back, check to see if they are secure before putting your baby in the seat.
- Stay within arm's reach of your baby when the seat is on any raised surface like a table. Never turn your back! Actually, the floor is the safest place for a baby in an infant seat.
- ABOVE ALL, NEVER USE AN INFANT SEAT AS A CAR SAFETY SEAT! It simply isn't designed to keep your baby safe if you're involved in an accident.

YOUR BABY'S CAR SAFETY SEAT

A car safety seat is absolutely the most important piece of baby equipment . . . and it's the most necessary! There are laws in all fifty states that require the use of a car safety seat whenever a child rides in a private automobile and in most states, that means any car, not just in his parents' car. You must even use a car safety seat for that first trip home from the hospital. In fact, some hospitals won't discharge your baby if you're going home by car and you don't have a seat.

Why is a car safety seat so necessary? The sad statistics show that car accidents, mostly on short trips, are a leading cause of serious injury and death among young children. Yet most of those children could have been saved if they were in a car safety seat or wearing a safety belt.

You might think that your infant is safe being held in your arms, as long as you wear your safety belt, and the car is driven slowly and carefully. It just isn't so! If the driver must suddenly brake or another car collides with yours, the force will wrench your baby from your arms and send him flying into the dashboard or windshield. Simulated tests have shown this happens even at speeds as low as 15 mph. It's just as dangerous to hold your baby in your lap and put the safety belt around both of you. In case of an accident or a sudden stop, your body would be pressed against the belt and your baby would absorb most of the force and suffer the most injury.

Fortunately, all car safety seats that have been manufactured since January 1981 are designed to meet a tough federal safety standard which includes passing a simulated crash test. Your baby is safest in one of these newer seats!

If you must use a seat made before 1981, you should contact the National Passenger Safety Association. (See Appendix.) Give the make and model number of the older seat and they will give you information on its safety and proper installation. If you don't have a seat, this organization may also be able to give you the name of a ''loaner'' program in your area that will loan you a car safety seat. You could also check with your local hospital or police department to find a ''loaner'' program.

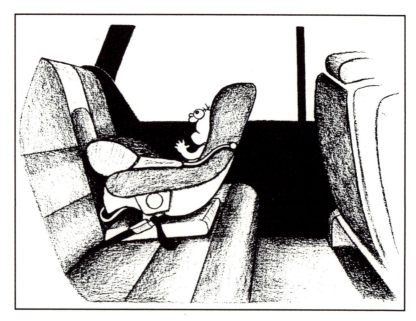

Buying A Car Safety Seat

Your first decision will be whether to buy an "infant-only" seat or a "convertible" seat that can be used into the toddler years.

An "infant" car safety seat can be used from birth until your baby weighs about twenty pounds. It can only be installed facing the rear of the car and is anchored by the car's safety belt. Your baby is then held in the seat with a harness.

Some seats have adjustable harness positions that will provide a secure fit for a small baby. (Note: Seats with lap shields are not recommended for premature infants because the shield would hit the baby in the face or neck.) Another advantage of an "infant" car safety seat is that you can easily remove and install it with the baby in place. Many of these seats can also be used as infant seats in the house. (BUT NEVER USE AN INFANT SEAT AS A CAR SAFETY SEAT, EVEN THOUGH THEY MAY LOOK SIMILAR.)

A "convertible" car safety seat is used in a reclining position, facing the back of the car, from birth until a baby is able to sit up straight. Then, the seat is adjusted to an upright position and turned around facing forward. It is designed to restrain a child weighing up to forty pounds.

These seats are anchored with the car's seat belt, although some may require an additional "tether." However, the tether type is difficult to install correctly and is not recommended unless it can be installed according to directions. There are many models and makes, and they differ depending on the type of harness and/or shield used to restrain the child. Choose one that you find easy to use. (Note: Before you buy either an infant or a convertible car safety seat, be sure that it can be installed correctly in your own car.)

Using Your Car Safety Seat Safely

A car safety seat will only provide adequate protection if you use it properly. Unfortunately, a recent study showed that three out of four seats are being used incorrectly!

- Always follow exactly the manufacturer's instructions for installing the seat. If you have questions, contact the manufacturer or the National Passenger Safety Association. (See Appendix.)

- If you have a seat that requires use of a tether, you must install it correctly.
- The safest place for the car seat is in the middle of the rear seat, where it is furthest from points of possible impact.
- If your baby is small, you can place a rolled-up towel or blanket around his head and sides for comfort.
- Adjust the harness so it fits your child snugly.
- Note: If the seat has restrained a child in a serious accident, it should be replaced since the frame may be weakened.

REMEMBER, ALWAYS SECURELY FASTEN YOUR BABY IN HIS CAR SAFETY SEAT WHENEVER HE IS IN THE CAR!

A STROLLER OR CARRIAGE

JOAN: Like so many other first-time parents, it never even occurred to us to question whether we needed a baby carriage. We just went out and bought the most solid and comfortable one we could find. I don't think Jamie rode in it more than half a dozen times and likewise with Lindsay. It was mainly used in the house, making it a very expensive bassinet! I finally started lending it out so I wouldn't feel as guilty about the cost.

For this baby, we bought a stroller that fully reclines, so it can take the place of a carriage for the first few months. It doesn't take up as much room and it's going to get a lot of use in the next couple years!

Now, when shopping for a stroller or carriage, you should always look for one that carries a seal, showing that it has met voluntary safety standards developed by the industry.

Some Safety Tips

- The stroller should have a base wide enough to prevent tipping, even when a baby leans over the side. If the seat can be adjusted to a reclining position, make sure the stroller cannot tip backward when a baby is lying down.

- If a stroller has a shopping basket for carrying packages, it should be low on the back of the stroller and in front of (or directly over) the rear wheels. Don't hang anything over the handles because the weight can cause the stroller to tip backwards . . . with your baby landing on his head!
- Check the seat belt to make sure it is strong and easy to fasten.
- The brake should be easy to operate and actually lock the wheels. Brakes on two wheels will provide extra safety.

A FRONT CARRIER

A front carrier is a cozy and convenient way for a mother (or father) to carry a baby, especially when shopping or working around the house. And it's natural for newborns to feel especially secure when they're held close to your body. (But remember, a back carrier should not be used until your baby is 6 months old and his neck is strong enough to withstand jolts.)

Here's what to look for when buying a front carrier:

- Are there wide shoulder straps that won't cut into your shoulders?
- Are the straps easily adjustable?
- Is it easy to put on and take off by yourself?
- Is there head and shoulder support for very young babies?
- Is it easy to wash?

YOUR BABY'S LAYETTE

JOAN: **I've finally learned to resist the powerful urge to buy loads of baby clothes . . . so should you! In the first place, if you don't know whether you'll have a boy or girl, you buy neutral whites and yellows which then tend to get ignored in favor of pink or blue. Also, baby clothes are a favorite gift . . . especially from grandmothers!**

If you look at the layette lists that are displayed in children's shops or infant departments, you might feel overwhelmed by how much there is to buy to keep your baby clothed and cozy. But keep in mind that these stores are in business to sell these items. How much you should buy actually depends on how often you plan to do laundry and how much you want to spend. So let's consider just the basic layette that your newborn really needs.

Undershirts. These come in three styles. The type that slip over the head will be the most difficult to use since your baby won't be able to hold his head up. The other styles are open in the front and close with either ties or snaps. Many people find the snaps easier to manage. You need six undershirts and it's smart to buy the six-month size—newborns grow quickly!

Diapers. There's no question about the necessity for diapers. Your only choice will be between the disposables and cloth diapers. Of course, the disposables are the most convenient and easier for novices to handle, but they are more expensive. Also, for some babies with particularly sensitive skin, disposable diapers might cause a rash.

Be especially careful when using the super absorbent type. They work so well at preventing leakage that you may not change the diapers often enough, and that can cause diaper rash.

As for the rumors that these super absorbent diapers may cause Toxic Shock Syndrome (TSS), investigations by the Centers for Disease Control, the U.S. Consumer Product Safety Commission and other agencies have found there is no link. Doctors point out that TSS bacteria only grow inside the body and diapers are worn externally.

If you decide on cloth diapers, the best type is a gauze weave that makes a very soft and absorbent diaper. The bird's eye weave wears longer but isn't as soft. If you use cloth diapers, you'll also need diaper pins, rubber or plastic pants and a diaper pail—one with a built-in deodorant holder!

JOAN: **Even if you use disposable diapers like we always have, it's a good idea to buy a couple dozen cloth diapers. They have all kinds of uses like protecting crib**

sheets and your clothing, just in case your baby spits up! And when the diapers are no longer needed for the baby, they still make great dust cloths.

Another alternative is a diaper service that provides cloth diapers and eliminates the hassle of washing diapers. Since they are sterilized, the diapers are less likely to cause a rash than ones washed in the home. Most diaper services are less expensive than using disposable diapers.

Nightgowns. To go over the undershirt and diapers, you can use nightgowns. You should start off with four, again in the six-month size. They may seem large at first, but your baby won't mind and he'll soon grow into them. Also, always remember when buying clothes for babies that it will be a lot easier to get the clothes on and off if they are a little too big. There's nothing more frustrating for parent and baby than trying to squeeze a head through a small opening or an arm into a narrow sleeve!

JOAN: **These nightgowns are my favorites for little babies, especially at night. It makes diaper changing and clean-up so easy—just loosen the tie, roll up the bottom and you're ready for business!**

Stretchies. These one-piece suits are a marvelous all-purpose way to dress your baby—he can sleep in them or go visiting. They are also easy to put on since they snap down the front. Just be careful each time you use them to check the inside of the feet for loose threads. If a thread wraps around a little toe, it can cut off circulation. You should start off with four stretchies in the six-month size.

Sweaters and Hats. A lightweight sweater is always handy, but whether your baby needs a heavy sweater or blanket sleeper depends on where you live and the season. However, a hat to cover your baby's head during outings is essential. If it's cold, a warm hat is necessary to keep him warm, since a baby can lose a large proportion of body warmth through an uncovered head. If it's sunny, try to keep your baby in the shade, but if you can't, put on a light hat with a brim to protect his head and shade his face.

Crib Sheets and Blankets.   You will need four crib sheets, preferably ones that have fitted corners and are the right size for the mattress. And to go under the sheet, get a couple yards of flannel-backed waterproof material that you can cut to size. It's washable and will protect the mattress. You should also buy a crib blanket and one for outings.

Receiving Blankets.   These small lightweight blankets are handy for many things like swaddling your baby or wrapping him up while changing clothes. Buy four good quality receiving blankets that will withstand many washings.

Now, once you've bought your basic layette, remember to bring one complete set of clothing and a receiving blanket to the hospital so your baby will have something to wear on his trip home!

JOAN: **And, speaking of packing things to take to the hospital, I have a little list of things I found useful and I give to friends of mine who are about to deliver. Often, expectant mothers get so involved planning for the baby they forget to think about what they need. Here are some things you should have packed and ready to go.**

- Two or three nightgowns—the shorties will make the frequent exams more comfortable for you and easier for your doctor and nurses. (I may as well warn you to leave your modesty at home! If you're planning to nurse your baby, choose nightgowns that button down the front or have stretchy tops.)
- You'll also need, if you're breastfeeding, a couple of nursing bras with detachable cups. When you buy them, allow enough room so they will be comfortable when your breasts are filled with milk.
- A bathrobe, slippers and toilet articles.
- If you have stitches, you can make them less uncomfortable by using a local anesthetic spray and hygenic wipes. Find out if these are available at your hospital and ask your doctor if there are any objections to using them. In any case, you should always ask for an ice pack as soon as you leave the

delivery room. Put it on your stitches and when it melts, ask for more ice. This will really help keep down the pain and swelling. Also, don't be afraid to ask for a painkiller if you feel you need one. There are several that may be used safely even if you are breastfeeding.

● Finally, bring along your own sanitary napkins because the hospital may only supply the old type that need a belt and pins.

Now, since a lot of ground has been covered in "preparing the nest," here are some quick checklists:

BABY EQUIPMENT CHECKLIST

CRIB, BASSINET or CRADLE .... ☐
CHANGING TABLE .... ☐
INFANT BATH TUB................................... ☐
INFANT SEAT... ☐
CAR SAFETY SEAT .... ☐
CARRIAGE or STROLLER........................... ☐
FRONT CARRIER..................................... ☐

BABY'S LAYETTE CHECKLIST

6 UNDERSHIRTS .... ☐
4 NIGHTGOWNS....................................... ☐
4 STRETCHIES .... ☐
1 SWEATER and HAT................................. ☐
DIAPERS .... ☐
4 CRIB SHEETS .... ☐
FLANNEL-BACKED WATERPROOF SHEETING . ☐
2 BLANKETS... ☐
4 RECEIVING BLANKETS .... ☐

JOAN'S HOSPITAL LIST FOR MOTHERS-TO-BE

2 or 3 SHORT NIGHTGOWNS .... ☐
2 NURSING BRAS..................................... ☐

BATHROBE and SLIPPERS........................... ☐
TOILET ARTICLES .... ☐
LOCAL ANESTHETIC SPRAY .... ☐
HYGIENIC WIPES .... ☐
SANITARY NAPKINS................................ ☐

CHAPTER 4
THE MAGIC MOMENT

NOW THAT YOU HAVE everything ready for the baby and the mother's bag is packed and ready to go, the big question is "Are you prepared to get to the hospital in a hurry, at anytime of the day or night?" Here's a checklist to help you:

- If you're going by taxi, keep the numbers of at least two cab companies by your telephone. Even if you live in a big city, you can't depend on finding a taxi cruising by your door when you need one.
- If you're driving to the hospital, plan out the shortest route and make a trial run, preferably at night, when signs are harder to read.
- Make sure you have change for tolls and keep plenty of gas in the car.

- Stay up to date on any road construction or other problems that could cause traffic jams or detours.

I learned this last advice the hard way—our second daughter, Lindsay, was almost born on the highway! We had moved to the suburbs, but our doctor and hospital were still in New York City. I had everything ready, but I had forgotten about a railroad strike that forced everyone to drive into the city. Joan's timing was perfect—her labor started just before the morning rush hour.

It was pure panic! I was weaving my way through traffic and at the same time trying to pretend I was calm while I helped Joan with Lamaze exercises. She was focusing on a little object on the dashboard and doing pretty well.

But when her contractions were two minutes apart and we were stuck on the West Side Highway, desperate measures were called for! I swung into the northbound lane (still driving southbound) and started blowing the horn. Sure enough, we attracted the attention of a police car. With sirens screaming, they escorted us to the hospital . . . and Joan delivered Lindsay just forty-five minutes later!

JOAN: **This time, since I was going to the same obstetrician, Dr. Hilliard Dubrow, and was planning to deliver at the same hospital, I was naturally a little apprehensive as my due date approached. But as it turned out, this trip to the hospital was planned ahead of time.**

When I went to my obstetrician two weeks before my due date, I mentioned that something seemed to be different. With my other two pregnancies I remembered getting kicked a lot up near my ribs, but now I was feeling kicks lower down, in the vaginal area. Upon examination he felt the baby was in a breech presentation and he immediately sent me for a sonogram. This confirmed a breech double footling presentation, that is, the baby's head was up and both feet were down. Another sonogram five days later showed little change in position and since the baby was estimated to be over eight pounds already, it wasn't likely that he or she would be able to spontaneously turn around so the head would be facing down.

Dr. Dubrow explained to us that a vaginal delivery could be dangerous to the baby. Normally the head descends first, opening up the delivery path as it goes. But now the feet and bottom would be delivered first, so the opening might not be wide enough by the time the head came through. The result could be injury to the baby's spine or brain. He said it was necessary to deliver the baby by cesarean section, before I went into labor, because of the possibility of rupturing the membranes and having the umbilical cord drop down. Since that was a Monday and my due date was only a week away, he scheduled the delivery for Thursday. Of course Michael and I were apprehensive, but we did have a leisurely drive to the hospital on Wednesday afternoon.

Another complication came up as a result of the necessity of a C-section. Our first two babies were normal vaginal deliveries and, having gone through the Lamaze program with Joan, I was in the delivery room both times coaching and supporting her. It meant very much to both of us that we be together at the incredible moment of our baby's birth. However, I soon discovered that our hospital has a different policy when it comes to a cesarean delivery. Fathers

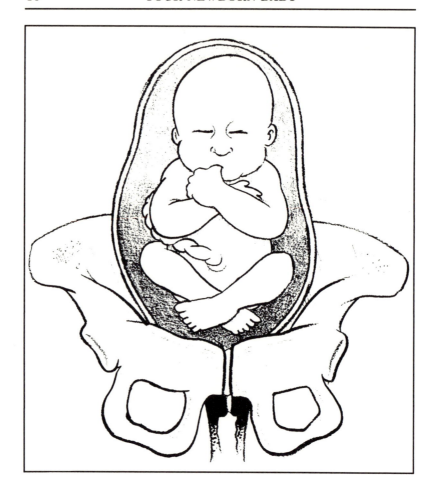

are not allowed in the delivery room. It seems that some guy was
a little faint-hearted . . . he keeled over and broke his nose!

In spite of our obstetrician's pleas, my reputation as a superior
coach and the fact the hospital plans to change the policy (they'll
install a special chair for fathers and will assign a nurse to stand
by), they would not allow me in the room with Joan. Naturally I
was very disappointed and it was a good lesson to check things like
this out well ahead of time.

However, I was able to be in the next room and there was an
intercom. It really helped relieve anxiety to know what was going
on and although I didn't see the moment of Sarah's birth, I was

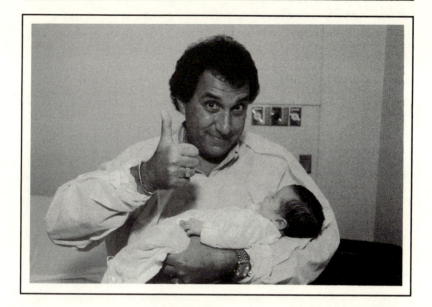

able to share in the excitement. Then, within five minutes, the nurse came out and handed me my new nine-pound-eight-ounce daughter. What an indescribable feeling!

Joan said she was so sure we were having a boy that she thought the doctor was kidding when he said "You have a big, beautiful, healthy, third baby girl!" . . . and then she was worried about how I would feel. To be honest, there was a moment of disappointment, but it was only a moment. As I held Sarah, the realization hit me that "while you know what you'd like, you love what you get . . . and I love this little girl!"

> JOAN: **I was awake and aware during the entire delivery since Dr. Dubrow had convinced me it was important for the baby's sake not to have general anesthesia—it crosses the placenta and can affect the baby. Instead, I had an epidural block and I'll admit I was very apprehensive about it. Now I'm happy I wasn't out cold. Not only was I able to see the baby as soon as she was born, but within an hour I was holding her in the recovery room and nursing her. I had nursed our other two girls right after delivery and I feel this is important in establishing breastfeeding.**

With this cesarean delivery, I was in a lot more pain and I really needed the nurse's help in positioning Sarah for breastfeeding. But it was worth it, especially since Sarah would also be getting bottles of glucose or sugar water. These are usually unnecessary and can confuse a baby who's trying to learn to breastfeed. However, the doctor explained that because Sarah was such a large baby she was more prone to a sharp drop in the level of her blood sugar and she needed the bottles. If I hadn't nursed her for the first day or two, she might have become so accustomed to being fed from a bottle that she didn't want to breastfeed. I'm happy to say that Sarah is a wonderful baby. She eats well and sleeps well!

CHAPTER 5
YOUR BABY FROM HEAD TO TOE

FINALLY! AFTER NINE MONTHS of anxious waiting, you get your first look at your precious newborn . . . and it's love at first sight! Then comes a closer examination and all the questions, especially from first-time parents. Of course, the most important question is "Is the baby healthy?" Your obstetrician or pediatrician will be able to reassure you and it's comforting to know that, according to the American Academy of Pediatrics, almost all newborns enter the world with no serious medical problems.

As to all the other questions that concerned Joan and me, like most new parents, about "What's normal?"—here are the answers we've gotten from our pediatrician, Dr. Brown, and the many other doctors we contacted in doing research. This is a complete guided tour of newborn babies . . . from head to toe!

THE HEAD

"Why are most babies born with such funny-shaped heads?"

When a baby travels down the birth canal, the bones in his head slide together, or even over each other, so by the time he finally emerges his head is elongated. This appearance may dismay some parents but it's normal and the baby's head will return to a nice round shape within a few weeks. Of course, in a cesarean birth in which the baby is lifted out through an incision in the uterus, the head will be round. In any case, don't be surprised by the large size of the baby's head—it's normally about one-fourth of baby's total length!

"Do babies usually have hair when they're born?"

Some babies are bald at birth and others come out looking like rock stars. Both styles are normal. But if your baby is born with hair, don't be concerned if it rubs off easily on the crib sheets or during baths. This first hair is very fine and brittle and it will grow back.

A newborn may also have some soft hair, called lanugo, covering his face and back. This doesn't mean you'll have a "hairy" child! The lanugo usually falls out in a few weeks but may take longer, so you may have to keep reassuring anxious grandparents.

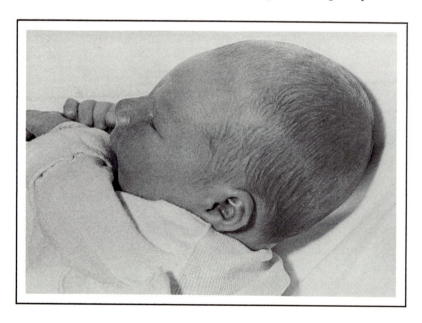

JOAN: **I was really surprised when I got my first look at Jamie—she was born with dark tight little curls all over her head. I just didn't expect to see all that hair!**

"What causes the soft spot on top of the baby's head, and is it alright to touch it?"

Actually, there are six soft spots, called fontanels, on the baby's head, and they are nature's way of allowing the baby's head to grow. The two small ones on each side and the small spot toward the back of the head will close up within a few months after birth. The diamond-shaped fontanel on the top of the head may be as large as two inches across and may not completely close until a baby is around eighteen months. It's normal for this spot to pulsate a little and it may also sink in slightly when the baby is sitting up quietly, or bulge slightly when the baby cries or is lying down.

JOAN: **Like many new parents, I was nervous at first about touching the large soft spot, especially when I was bathing the scalp. I felt the baby's brain was right underneath the skin and I could damage it if I pressed too hard. My doctor reassured me that a baby's brain is well-protected by a layer of fluid and the area is**

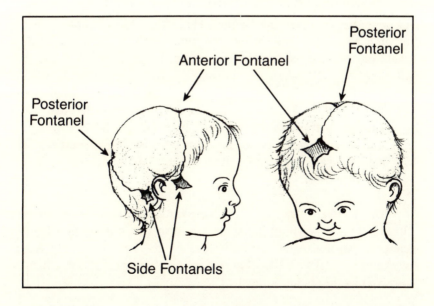

**covered by a tough membrane that eventually turns
into bone. In fact, he said it's a good idea to become
familiar with the normal feel of the soft spot. Then
you'll be able to tell the difference if the fontanel bulges
and feels tense at a time when your baby is ill. This is
a signal to call your doctor at once!**

THE EYES

"How well can a newborn really see people or things?"

In the hour or so just after birth, it's common for newborns
to be wide-eyed and alert, checking out their new world and their
new parents. This first eye contact is so exciting for parents and
it's an important part of the bonding process. (The use of silver
nitrate drops to prevent eye infections has been criticized as being
too irritating to the eye, and there is alternative treatment. See
Chapter 2.)

Actually, newborns can see quite well but their clearest focus
point is when objects or people are about eight to ten inches away.
It's no coincidence that this is the distance from the mother's breast
to her face!

Babies will also follow moving objects at this distance (so don't
hang mobiles three feet away). And it's not true that newborns only
see in terms of black and white. They not only see colors, but
research has shown that babies are more likely to be attracted to
bright colors, like red and yellow, and to large patterns instead of
solids.

> JOAN: **Before I learned this, we decorated Jamie and
> Lindsay's nursery all in white and soft pastels. Now
> our new nursery is an absolute riot of the primary
> colors—red, blue and yellow. Sarah has lots to catch
> her attention.**

Dr. T. Berry Brazelton, the well-known pediatrician who has
closely studied newborn behavior, has also found out that a baby
learns to recognize his mother's face by the time he's only two
weeks old. It takes a little longer, around four weeks, for a baby
to recognize his father's face!

"Why aren't the whites of the eye clear?"

Newborns often have blood spots or hemorrhages in the white of the eye due to the breaking of little blood vessels during delivery. These spots usually disappear in a week or so. The white area of the eye, called the sclera, may also appear bluish at first because the underlying dark layer, called the choroid, shines through the thin sclera.

"How long will it be before we know the color of her eyes?"

Most Caucasian infants are born with blue-gray irises and most black infants have brown-gray irises. Unless the baby's genes call for blue or green eyes, the color will slowly darken and most babies have their final eye color by the time they are one year old.

"Why does the baby have crossed eyes?"

With most newborns, the crossed-eye look is really an illusion caused by the wide space between the eyes and a fold of skin that hides the inner area of the white of the eye. Your doctor can use a bright light to check whether there is any true misalignment of the pupils. In either case, crossed eyes usually straighten out by the time a baby is 3 months old. If the condition still persists, your baby should have a thorough examination by an ophthamologist. The earlier he's treated, the better.

"Why aren't there tears when the baby cries?"

Even though all babies do a lot of crying, it's normal not to produce tears for the first few weeks. Then the tears should drain from the inside corner of the eyes into the nose through the tear ducts. You notice tears when there are too many for the ducts to handle, and the eyes fill up with water and overflow. Occasionally, one or both ducts don't open or become blocked. If you see your baby's eyes tearing constantly or there's yellowish discharge, you should call your doctor.

THE NOSE

"Is a baby supposed to breathe through her nose or her mouth, or doesn't it matter?"

Newborn babies breathe through their noses, so if you see your

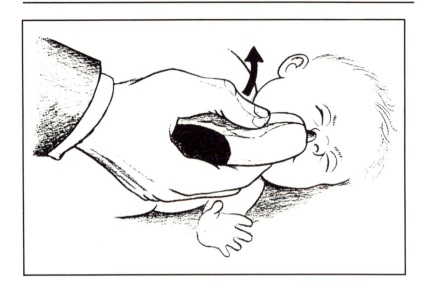

baby breathing through her mouth, it usually means the nose is clogged.

> JOAN: **Dr. Brown said we could gently try to remove any debris with a cotton swab, but if the baby has a bad cold and the nose is really stuffy, he recommended using a nasal aspirator with a soft tip. This is a tube with a large rubber bulb on the end that works like a nose dropper, but in reverse. You must be very careful to squeeze the bulb BEFORE putting the end of the tube in the baby's nostril. If you squeeze the bulb when the tube is in the nostril, the air will force the mucous deeper into the nasal passages. Then, as you gently release the bulb, the mucous is suctioned out of the nose.**

"What does it mean when a baby sneezes?"

Sneezing isn't always an indication of a cold so don't rush to bundle the baby up in blankets. Sometimes it's just the only way a baby has of clearing her nose of dried mucous and dust. If you live in a dry climate or have heat on during the winter, it's a good idea to keep a humidifier going in the baby's room to add some moisture to the air.

JOAN: **We prefer the cool-mist type of humidifier because the kind that produces steam could be dangerous if one of the girls got too close. But you must be careful to clean the humidifier every week or so. Otherwise, organisms could grow on the inside of the unit and get misted into the air.**

"Why does the baby's nose seem to be lopsided?"

Again, the trip down the birth canal is a rough one and the newborn's nose can get a little pushed to the side. It will straighten out in time. But if the septum, or partition in the middle of the nose, is twisted or dislocated, your baby's doctor will need to correct it.

THE EARS

"Why are the baby's ears folded forward? Does that mean her ears will stick out?"

A newborn's ears may be folded toward the face because they were positioned that way in the tightly packed uterus and they will gradually straighten out now that there's room. This is not a cause of protruding ears which is usually an inherited trait.

"How well can a baby hear?"

A newborn baby should have excellent hearing and often responds to even soft sounds with a jerking motion of the whole body. Parents often worry that their baby's nervous system is too sensitive, but this is really a normal reaction to a sudden noise or movement. It's called the Moro, or "startle" reflex and it's a good indicator that your baby has normal hearing. A baby will jerk his legs up, throw his arms out and then bring them close to his body. The reflex doesn't do much to protect the baby, but your doctor will use the symmetry of movement as a way of testing the baby's neurologic system. After the first couple weeks, this reflex gradually disappears.

In fact, the experts say that even before birth, a baby can hear the mother's heartbeat as well as sounds outside the womb . . . and we have proof! When Joan was pregnant with Jamie, I would get really close to where I thought the baby's head was positioned and say, "This is your father talking." And, since I'm also a musician,

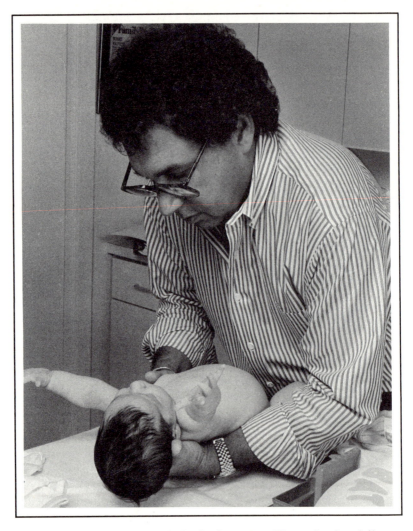

I sang a little sequence of rhythmic notes. Then, in the delivery room, moments after Jamie was born and she was screaming her head off, I held her and went into the same routine. She quieted down immediately! It was very moving and the doctors and nurses were really impressed. The same thing happened when I sang to our new baby, Sarah.

"Is it necessary to clean the baby's ears?"
    There's no need to clean the ears, but many parents do it so their baby's appearance is more socially acceptable.

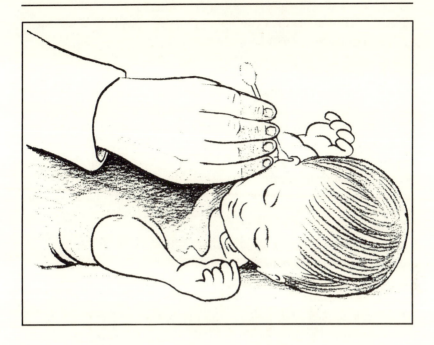

JOAN: **Since I'm one of those parents, Dr. Brown showed me an easy and safe technique. After the baby's bath, you take a cotton swab and rest your hand on the baby's cheek while you clean ONLY the outer area of the ear. That way, if the baby moves suddenly, your hand moves with her and there's less chance of the swab getting pushed into the ear. You must NEVER try to clean the inside area of the ear canal.**

THE MOUTH

"What should I do about white patches in the baby's mouth?"

Sometimes, milk that remains in a baby's mouth will curdle and leave white patches on the tongue or cheeks. You should be able to wipe it off easily with a handkerchief or piece of gauze. But if the white patch is difficult to remove or a little comes off leaving an area that's red or bleeding, your baby probably has a yeast infection called "thrush." Call your doctor so he can prescribe medication. It's important to clear up a thrush infection quickly because, left untreated, it can travel through your baby's digestive system and cause a nasty diaper rash!

"Why are there little bumps on the baby's gums?"

It's common for newborns to have some round white or yellowish bumps on the gums (called Bohn's pearls) or on the roof of the mouth (Epstein's pearls). The gum bumps may be mistaken for teeth, but they feel softer and smoother than teeth. These bumps are caused by a cheesy material that is produced by oil glands and they will disappear by three months. By the way, a small percentage of babies are born with a few teeth. They are nothing to worry about although they may intimidate a nursing mother!

"Why does the baby's tongue seem to protrude? Is it too large?"

When a baby is relaxed, it's normal for the mouth to fall open and the tongue may dangle out a bit.

"What causes the blister on the baby's lip and should it be treated?"

Both breastfed and bottle-fed babies may get a little blister in the middle of their upper lip. It comes from all the sucking, especially if the baby really works hard.

> JOAN: **Each of our babies had one of these sucking blisters, but the doctor said it doesn't hurt and there's no need to put anything on it.**

THE CHEST

"Why do the baby's nipples seem to be swollen?"

Most newborns, both boys and girls, are born with breast tissue that makes the nipples appear swollen. The tissue is a result of both the mother's milk-producing hormones and the baby's own hormones. These breasts actually do produce milk which can be expressed by squeezing the nipple—BUT DON'T DO IT, even out of curiosity, since this will stimulate the breast to produce even more milk. In the past, this milk used to scare people and they called it "witches' milk." Although this breast tissue will gradually diminish over the next month or so, it may take up to a year before it disappears completely. However, if you notice new swelling and the nipples look red or sore, there may be an infection, so call your doctor.

"Is it possible for a baby to have more than two nipples?"

Yes, it's possible, but fairly uncommon. During the embryonic stage, all mammals have a line of nipples going down each side of the torso. In the human species, all but two of these nipples will disappear. But sometimes there's an oversight and an extra nipple might be left, usually just below one or both of the normal nipples. There is rarely any breast tissue underneath and it may be mistaken for a light brown mole.

"Why does the baby's heart seem to be racing?"

It's normal for a newborn's heart to beat more quickly. The range is ninety to one hundred and fifty times a minute, around fifty percent faster than the normal range for an adult! Since a newborn's weight is small compared to his surface area, his metabolism has to work faster. This is also a reason an infant normally breathes faster than an older child or an adult.

You may also notice variations in the baby's heartbeat that are caused by the newborn's immature nervous system. The beat may slow down dramatically when the baby moves his bowels, yawns or has a hiccup attack. Then it returns to the normal rate.

> JOAN: **What scared me was I could actually see, or at least feel, the baby's heart pumping away so fast. It looked like the baby was in distress. But the doctor pointed out that a newborn's chest wall is quite thin and the heart was just performing normally.**

"Why does a baby's heart sound different from an adult's?"

If you've been listening to your baby's heartbeat during pregnancy, you'll recognize the same even tick-tocking sound in your newborn. It isn't the same as the short-long sound made by the heart of an older infant or an adult. Parents who are curious enough to use a stethoscope might also become concerned by murmuring sounds issuing from the baby's heart. Fortunately, most of these murmurs are caused by the normal development of the newborn's respiratory and circulatory systems as they adjust to life outside the womb, but if you're anxious, ask your doctor to give a listen.

"What can be done to stop the baby's hiccups?"

There are many home remedies, such as breathing into a paper bag or swallowing sugar. OBVIOUSLY NONE OF THESE SHOULD BE USED ON AN INFANT! But don't worry, most babies hiccup, even before they are born, and it's not necessary to do anything about the hiccups—the baby really doesn't mind them! Of course, if they go on for days and interfere with eating and sleeping, you should check with your doctor.

As to the cause of the hiccups, no one has the final answer. One theory is that the vagus nerve in the back of the throat is irritated—another theory puts the blame on air swallowed during feeding.

THE NAVEL

"What determines whether a navel will be an 'inny' or an 'outy'?"

After delivery, the baby no longer needs nourishment from the placenta so the umbilical cord is clamped and cut. Doctors frequently have to reassure parents that the position of the clamp has nothing to do with whether their child's navel will be an "inny" or an "outy." In fact, the navel's final appearance is determined by the same thing that shapes the baby's ears—genetics!

"What kind of care does the umbilical stump need?"

In most newborn nurseries, the raw end of the cord is painted with an antiseptic to help prevent infection. Once home, the only care necessary is to expose the stump to the air as much as possible and avoid getting it wet—some doctors advise only sponge baths during this time. The stump gradually becomes hard and brown, like a scab, and usually falls off within two weeks. Then, if there is any bleeding or oozing, a little alcohol can be applied with a cotton swab. If, at any time, you notice a foul odor, swelling or a spreading area of redness indicating an infection, call your doctor.

> JOAN: **When Jamie was born, the baby nurse used to tuck her diapers down in the front. I thought that was the way to diaper a baby so I kept it up for months until her doctor pointed out the only reason for doing it was to keep the umbilical stump and the navel dry so it healed quickly.**

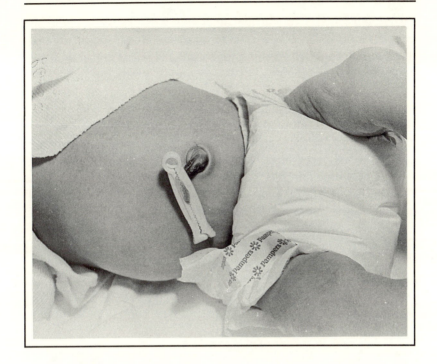

"What causes a bump or bulge in the area of the navel?"

This is called an umbilical hernia and it's caused by part of an organ or the intestine protruding through an opening in the abdominal muscles. It may be more noticeable when the baby cries or strains during a bowel movement . . . but don't worry! These hernias aren't painful and most of them disappear as the opening spontaneously closes, usually by the end of the first year. Parents shouldn't try to reduce the hernia by placing tape or a binding over the area. It won't help and may even create other problems!

THE GENITALS

"Is it normal for a girl's genitals to appear swollen?"

Many girls are born with very prominent labia minora, the inner lips of the genitals. These have been stimulated by the mother's hormones, especially estrogen, that were produced during pregnancy. As the effect of the hormones wear off, the inner lips will return to normal size and the outer lips will gradually cover the area. You may also notice a white, or even a bloody, discharge for the first few days. This is a normal hormonal reaction that indicates your baby's reproductive tract is functioning properly.

"Why do some baby boys have such large testicles?"

The testicles are really normal in size, but extra fluid has been trapped in the sac that surrounds them. It's called a hydrocele and is often a source of bragging by the baby's father. However, by the end of three months or so, the fluid is usually absorbed into the body and the jokes end. So if you want to show the baby off, the first few weeks are a good time to do it!

"How do you care for a circumcision and how can you tell if it's infected?"

The circumcised area is normally swollen and is covered with a wet scab that may frequently break off. It may look terrible but usually isn't infected. The problem is that it's difficult to keep the wound dry because it's often in contact with the diaper contents. You can help the healing along by coating the area with a little petroleum jelly and changing the diapers as soon as they're soiled. However, if you notice the area is red, warm or there's a yellowish discharge, these are signs of infection and you should call your doctor.

"What if the baby isn't circumcised, how do you keep the penis clean?"

The Academy of Pediatrics warns parents against cleaning underneath the foreskin, "Do not try to retract the foreskin in an infant, as it is almost always attached to the glans." Not only will it hurt, but any tearing of the tissue might cause scarring that may later prevent the foreskin from separating naturally. (See p. 14.)

They recommend cleaning the external area the same way as you do any other part of the body, "An uncircumcised penis does not need any special care." You may notice a whitish cheesy material that comes from under the foreskin or even seems trapped between the glans and the foreskin. This is a normal combination of shedding skin cells and secretions, called smegma.

THE HIPS, LEGS AND FEET

"The baby's legs seem so loose in the hip joints—is that normal?"

This "looseness" in newborn's hips may make them appear to be dislocated, but it is really caused by the mother's hormone, relaxin, crossing over via the placenta. The relaxin softens the supporting tissues around the joints, giving the mother loose hips so she can deliver more easily. The condition will disappear as the hormone fades from the baby's body.

The doctor should always check the baby's hips to determine whether there is any actual hip dislocation which would require early treatment. For mild cases, doctors often recommend double or triple diapering to hold the baby's legs at the proper angle until the joints stabilize.

"Why are a baby's legs curved in so much?"

That's the position they were forced into during the last few months inside the womb—the familiar fetal position. It's often referred to as "tibular bowing."

This tight fit may also cause a baby's feet to turn upward, inward or outward. Everything usually straightens out by the time a baby is around fifteen months old. The exception is clubfoot in which the foot bends down so the baby would be walking on the inside of the foot. This condition requires medical correction.

"Why is the baby's heel red and sore-looking?"

It is routine in hospital nurseries to prick the baby's heel so his blood can be tested for PKU, a disease which, if left untreated, can result in mental retardation. This important test is usually done on the third day after birth, so if you leave the hospital earlier or deliver your baby at home, ask your doctor to do the blood test as soon as possible.

"What causes a baby's toes to be so crooked, or even webbed?"

Again, it's that crowded womb that creates crooked and over-lapping toes, but they eventually straighten out. Webbing between the toes, or sometimes fingers, is a different story. This happens during fetal development when the skin doesn't separate completely, and the condition seems to run in certain families.

THE SKIN

Now that you've had a thorough look at a newborn baby from head to toe, it's time to examine the overall packaging—his skin.

> JOAN: **And here's where you're really in for a surprise. You know the expression "smooth as a baby's skin" or the image of "baby pink"—well, it doesn't apply to a newborn's skin!**

First of all, there's the color. A baby emerges from the womb looking rather grayish and covered with a white cheesy material, called vernix caseosa, which may be washed off or rubbed into the baby's skin. This protective coating is a great conditioner! Then, as soon as the baby takes his first breaths and the oxygen level of his blood increases, his color rapidly turns to pink and then reddish. This ruddy complexion is most noticeable in light-skinned babies, but after a few hours the skin will settle down to a more normal color. However, there are times your baby's skin may still assume different colors.

> ***Purplish mottling.*** You may notice this when you're changing or bathing your baby. It's caused by the small veins near the skin dilating when the baby is chilled.

Blue hands and feet. This may be caused by immature circulation or chilling and will disappear when the baby is warmed. However, if the bluish color persists or covers the entire body, it could be a sign of a serious heart or respiratory condition, so call your doctor!

Half-red/half-white. If your baby has been lying on his side, you may be startled by a "harlequin" effect. The downward half of his skin is bright red and the upward half is white, as if a line has been drawn down the middle of his body! This is caused by immature circulation during the first few weeks and will disappear when the baby changes position or begins to cry.

Mongolian blue spots. These areas of bluish color are accumulations of pigment that are often seen on the buttocks but may occur on other parts of the body. They usually disappear in two or three years and are no cause for concern. The spots are NOT bruises, symptoms of blood diseases, nor are they related to Down's syndrome, often incorrectly referred to as "Mongolism." In fact, doctors no longer use this term.

Yellow. By the second or third day of life, about half of all newborns turn yellow, including the whites of their eyes. This normal condition is called jaundice and is caused by a build-up of a substance, bilirubin (pronounced "Billy Rubin"), in the blood. As the baby's excess red blood cells are destroyed, bilirubin is formed which must be processed by the liver so it can be excreted. The problem comes when the immature liver can't get rid of all the bilirubin and the excess results in the skin's yellow color. After a few days, when the liver starts working up to speed, the jaundice disappears, and it doesn't recur.

During this time, your doctor will carefully monitor the level of bilirubin. If it rises, it can be lowered by exposing the baby to special lights. This is important because extreme amounts of bilirubin can put a baby at risk of developing a type of brain injury. However, most cases of jaundice are mild and there is no reason to stop breastfeeding.

There is a type of jaundice, called breast-milk jaundice, that affects one to two percent of nursing infants. No one knows why, but breastfeeding seems to prolong jaundice or increase the level of bilirubin. The recommendation is to temporarily stop nursing for forty-eight hours. This lowers the bilirubin level and the condition eventually clears up.

Rashes, spots and bumps

JOAN: **Then, just as the baby's color is improving, come the rashes, spots and bumps. It seemed as if our babies always looked just fine until it was time for a special visit, then their skin would break out with a vengeance! Here are the more common conditions that don't require any special treatment:**

Little yellow or white bumps.   These are called "milia" and usually appear on the oily parts of the face. They are filled with a cheesy material produced by the oil glands and will disappear by themselves within three months—don't squeeze!

Hives with white spots in the middle.   This is so common it's called "newborn rash." It can appear anywhere on the baby's body—usually whenever you're about to show off your beautiful baby to friends and relatives. Reassure them that it's not an allergy, and it's not flea bites! The red spots may even form blisters and look like they're infected. If they grow rapidly, ask your doctor to have a look. After a few weeks, when everyone's seen the baby, this rash goes away for good.

Pink pimples.   If you think back to your adolescent years, you'll recognize these pimples. It's called "baby acne" and is caused by the same overactive oil glands. This time they're stimulated by a combination of the baby's and the mother's hormone, testosterone. Since this is primarily a male hormone, baby boys may have a more severe case than baby girls. Don't use any of the teenage acne preparations—they are too strong for the baby's new skin. You can try drying the pimples by gently patting the area with cornstarch. This will create an interesting effect of a white face with red spots, so don't plan on taking any color pictures!

Tiny red spots. This is the familiar "prickly heat" that results from the tendency of a newborn baby's sweat glands to become blocked. It's most common on the face, neck, chest and in the bends of the arms and legs.

> JOAN: **I learned the hard way that a baby who is wrapped up too warmly is more likely to sweat and get prickly heat. Remember that your baby only needs to be dressed as you do—if you don't need to wear a heavy sweater in the middle of summer, neither does he!**

And to top it all off, don't be surprised if your baby's skin starts peeling during the first week or so. This is a normal shedding of dead skin cells! But take heart and be patient. Eventually your baby's skin color will take on its normal hue and the texture will be deliciously soft and smooth—it just may take a few months!

CHAPTER 6
FEEDING YOUR BABY

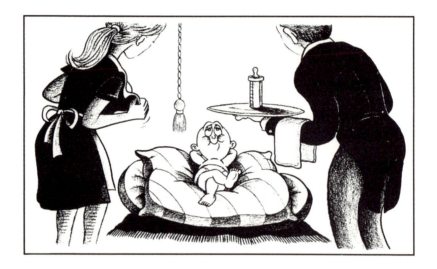

ONCE PARENTS ARE REASSURED their newborn is normal and everything's in good working order, the major concern becomes feeding their baby. Actually it's a lot simpler than seems to be indicated by the length of this chapter! For at least the first four months, there are only two choices, breast milk or formula, and all the experts agree that breast milk is best for babies. (See Chapter 2, Breast or Bottle.)

- If you decide not to breastfeed your baby, or must stop for some reason, commercial infant formula is an acceptable alternative. Its composition is designed to be as close as possible to breast milk and it has been processed so it's more digestible and less likely to cause allergies than cow's milk.

  The American Academy of Pediatrics recommends that

commercial infant formula be given until a baby is AT LEAST SIX MONTHS OLD. After that age, many doctors allow switching to pasteurized whole milk.

- The American Academy of Pediatrics does not recommend using homemade formulas prepared from evaporated milk or any other kind of milk. They lack the necessary amounts of certain nutrients.
- Solid food or juice is not recommended by the Academy before a baby is at least four months old, preferably six months. Solids put more strain on a baby's digestive system and may make him more susceptible to food allergies . . . and they WON'T help him sleep through the night!

Now, whether you breastfeed or formula-feed your baby, here's the most important thing to keep in mind. EACH BABY IS AN INDIVIDUAL . . . especially when it comes to eating! Some newborns might take a little longer than others to work up an appetite. And just like older children and adults, they don't always feel like eating the same amounts every day. So relax and don't compare your baby's eating habits with those of his siblings or the baby next door!

BREASTFEEDING YOUR BABY

JOAN: **By the time your baby is born, you will have made your decision about breast or formula—hopefully in favor of breastfeeding! I nursed all three babies and I'm really glad I did. But you may be feeling a little apprehensive. I remember that before Jamie was born, one of the biggest fears I had concerned breastfeeding—"Would I be able to do it?" "Would it seem weird?"**

Since I feel strongly that the best way to relieve anxiety is through information, my way of coping was to really do my homework and I read everything I could find on breastfeeding! I realized that it is a natural process that you learn along with your baby. The most important thing you can do is to be informed and to relax! So in the following section I'd like to pass along everything I've learned—from books, other

nursing mothers and hands-on experience—about the basics of breastfeeding your baby!

THE "LETDOWN REFLEX"

The best place to begin is by understanding how your breasts produce milk. During pregnancy your breasts have become two to three times heavier as the milk glands increase. These grape-like

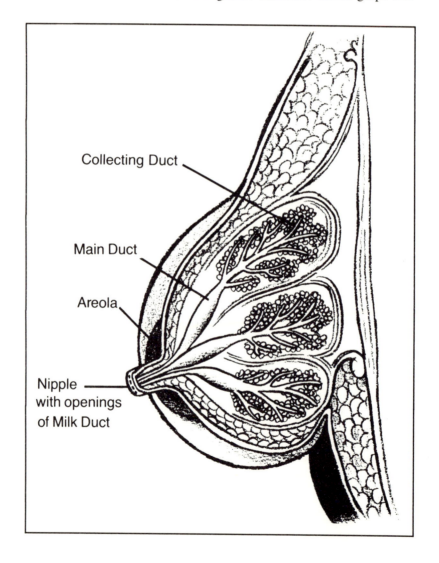

Collecting Duct

Main Duct

Areola

Nipple with openings of Milk Duct

clusters are where the milk is produced. The milk then drains into ducts which empty into milk reservoirs or sinuses that lie beneath the areola (the pigmented area surrounding the nipple). Each sinus is connected to an opening in the nipple—there are between fifteen and twenty openings. When your baby begins to nurse, this is what happens:

1. Nerves within the nipple are stimulated and a message is sent to the brain's pituitary gland.
2. A hormone (oxytocin) is released that contracts the tissue around the milk glands. Another hormone (prolactin) that stimulates the glands to produce milk is also released.
3. The milk drains into the sinuses and out through the openings in the nipples.

The whole process takes two to three minutes. It's called the "letdown reflex." You will usually feel your breasts become full and the area around the areolas and nipples will tingle. (Some mothers never have this feeling, even though they are "letting-down.") This reflex can also be inhibited by pain, emotional stress or extreme fatigue. That's why it's so important to stay relaxed and get as much rest as possible.

Once breastfeeding is established, the "letdown reflex" can occur in response to other stimuli such as hearing any infant cry, the sight of another baby or during intercourse. Mothers who are away from their babies often claim they have a sixth sense when their babies are crying and will "letdown." What's happening is that the baby and the mother are on the same internal "timer" that signals a feeding.

JOAN: **I was still nursing after I went back to work and this happened to me one time I was interviewing an important U.S. Senator on "Good Morning America"! I could feel the milk leaking through and right after the interview I dashed into the dressing room to dry my blouse with a hair dryer! I just made it back in front of the camera in time for my next segment.**

I learned it's a good idea to even double up on the nursing pads you wear inside your bra. By the way, when I was shopping for things before the new

baby, someone said the nursing pads weren't really necessary. Don't believe it! Some actually offer better protection than others, so it's worth experimenting.

TYPES OF BREAST MILK

The first milk that you produce is called colostrum. It is thick, yellow and rich in vitamins, minerals, protein and immunities that help prevent infections. Colostrum, even though it looks creamy, is lower in fat than formulas—one reason breastfed babies tend to lose a little weight after birth. It also helps the infant pass his first stools, called meconium, and research indicates that the sooner meconium is out of the baby's system, the less chance of developing jaundice.

After the fifth day, transition milk is produced, which has more calories. Somewhere around the fifteenth day, mature milk starts to come in. Don't worry if it appears to be thin, with a bluish tinge —it is rich in all the nutrients your baby needs!

GETTING STARTED

For countless generations, when babies were born at home, they were put to the mother's breast soon after delivery. Then as hospital births became the norm, a series of routine procedures tended to separate the mother and baby for the first few hours. However, current research has shown the advantages of early nursing and it's become common practice in many hospitals to allow babies to breastfeed as soon as possible after delivery.

Your baby is born with a sucking reflex and it's strongest in the first hour, during the baby's quiet alert stage. Then it's normal for a baby to go into a sleepy stage without much interest in eating for a while. He may not have gotten much during this first feeding, but at least he has the idea of where to find his food supply!

This early nursing also helps you! Your baby's sucking or even licking the nipple helps to stimulate the release of the hormones that produce colostrum. One of the hormones, oxytocin, also causes uterine contractions. This can lessen postpartum bleeding and it gets your uterus back into its non-pregnant state more quickly. As you nurse, you can actually feel your uterus contracting—a strange sensation that may be a little uncomfortable, but it's another example of how well the whole system is designed!

But what if you have to deliver your baby through cesarean section . . . how soon can you nurse? If you've had an epidural or spinal anesthetic, your baby can be put to your breast soon after delivery. With a general anesthetic you must wait until the effects have worn off and then help may be needed in holding your baby. Most pain medication that is prescribed after delivery will not affect a baby through breast milk.

THE BASICS OF BREASTFEEDING

JOAN: When breastfeeding was commonplace and people lived in extended families, there was always an "old hand" around to instruct the new mother and help with any problems. Now, a hospital nurse may give you some advice, but in two or three days you're home and on your own. Fortunately, there's an organization, La Leche League International, whose purpose is to provide advice on *The Womanly Art of Breastfeeding* as their excellent book is named. In many areas, local groups hold meetings where you can learn from the experiences and suggestions of other nursing mothers. If you need help in finding the nearest group or want more information, you can write or call their main office—they even have a hot-line number! (See Appendix.)

Now, to get you started, here are La Leche League's recommendations on basic breastfeeding technique that are based on the latest research:

1. Wash your hands with soap and water, but not your breast— too much washing can cause your nipples to dry and crack.

2. Position yourself so you are most comfortable—pain and tension can inhibit letdown. Sitting up in bed or in a rocking chair is usually the easiest, with plenty of pillows to support your back and the arm that is holding the baby. It helps to put your feet up on something or rest them on a footstool.

- Don't nurse your baby in a hunched-over position—your back will start to protest.
- If you cannot sit up, you can nurse while lying on your side—place a pillow behind your back.

3. It's very important to position your baby properly. The pillow in your lap should raise him to the level of your breast. Nestle him in your arm so that his neck rests in the bend of your elbow, his back is along your forearm and his buttocks are in your hand. Turn your baby's entire body so he is facing you. Tuck his lower arm

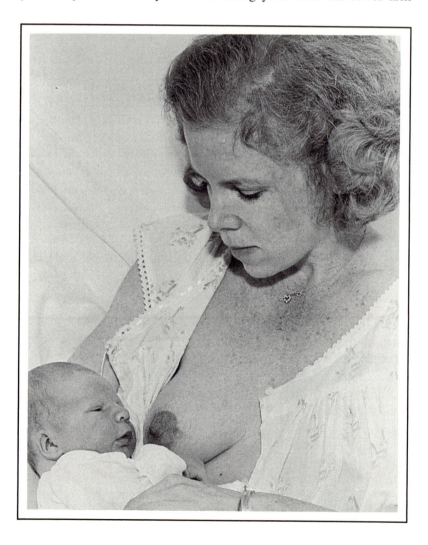

between him and your midriff close to your body. This is called the "cradle hold."

- Your baby should not have to turn his head or strain his neck to reach the nipple. It should be right in front of his mouth.
- Don't allow his head to tilt backward—milk could be forced into his middle ear.

4. Cup your breast with the other hand, supporting it with your fingers underneath and your thumb on top. This helps a newborn

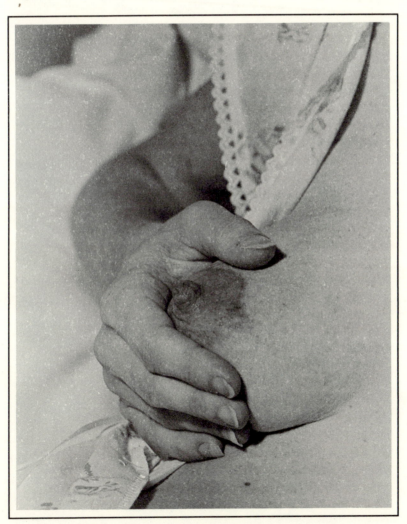

who hasn't a strong enough suction to hold the breast in his mouth by himself.

- Your fingers should not be touching the areola. This prevents the baby from placing his jaws on the areola.

5.   Tease the baby's mouth open by gently tickling his lips with your nipple. You can also tempt him by expressing a little milk to moisten the nipple.

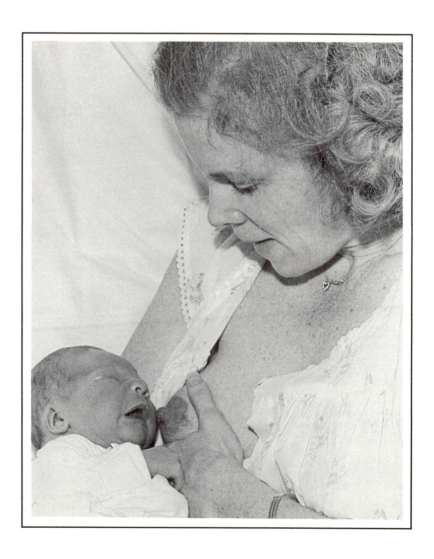

- Don't mash the baby's lips—he may not recognize the signal.
- Don't touch the baby's cheek or side of the head to push him toward the nipple. Babies have a rooting reflex that causes them to turn toward any touch—in this it would be away from the nipple.

6. Here comes the most important part! As soon as your baby opens his mouth wide, like a baby bird, center the nipple and quickly

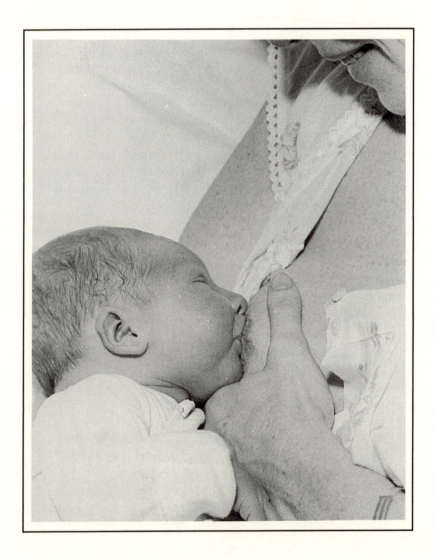

pull him in close with the arm that's holding him. This way he will latch on to the areola where the milk sinuses are. The tip of his nose should touch your breast. Don't worry that he won't be able to breathe. He'll get air from the sides of his nose or if your breast is very full, you can use your thumb and press gently on the breast to uncover his nose.

- Don't worry about getting all the areola in his mouth. If it's a large area, this won't be possible.
- Don't allow the baby to latch on only to your nipple. Not only won't he be getting enough milk, but you're likely to get sore nipples. If this happens, remove him and try again.
- Make sure he isn't pulling in his lower lip as he sucks. If he is, gently pull out his lip after he begins to nurse.
- If your breast is so engorged with milk that the baby can't get a proper hold on the areola, hand express a little milk so the area becomes softer. (See Expressing Milk.)

JOAN: Even after "toughening up" my nipples, that first sensation when the baby "latched-on" was enough to make my toes curl! But it doesn't last very long and you do get used to it.

7. To remove the baby from the nipple, break the suction by placing your little finger in the corner of his mouth.

- Don't pull him off—that hurts the nipple!

8. Give him a chance to burp, although babies don't always need to. (See p. 91, Burping Your Baby.) It's okay to wake him up if he's sleepy and then switch to the other breast. At each feeding you should always start with the alternate breast. That way each breast has the opportunity to be completely emptied at least every other feeding. This is important in preventing infections.

JOAN: It's really easy to forget, so after each feeding, I put a little safety pin on my bra strap to remind myself which breast to start with next time.

You can see that done properly, breastfeeding is pretty uncomplicated. Remember, it's important to relax and enjoy this wonderful time with your baby.

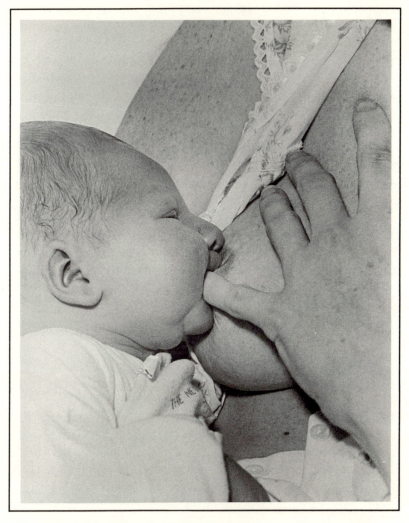

And if you feel you're getting a little too much well-meaning advice, don't be afraid to ask for some privacy. This is really a process that you and your baby will work out together. Don't worry if he or she doesn't get the hang of it right away. Some babies are born as if they had been nursing for months and others take a little while to learn. Just don't rush to give him bottles of water, formula or breast milk. The different nipple and sucking technique may cause confusion and could interfere with learning to nurse.

HOW OFTEN

Breastfeeding follows the basic principle of SUPPLY AND DEMAND. In the beginning, your body does not know how much milk your baby needs. But the more often your baby nurses, the more milk you will produce. The less often you nurse, the less milk. Since breast milk is produced almost continuously, you don't have to wait for your breasts to fill up!

When your milk supply is being established, the most important thing is to feed your baby whenever he's hungry. That means "demand feeding," not trying to follow any schedule. Breast milk is digested more quickly than formula so most newborns need to nurse at least every two to three hours . . . some even more frequently. Don't be tempted into having someone else give a relief bottle of formula during this time—not only can it confuse your baby, but he may not be hungry enough at the next feeding. You may have to become an expert at catnaps, but try to remember that your baby will eventually settle down to longer intervals.

HOW LONG

For the first few days, some doctors recommend limiting the amount of time a baby nurses at each feeding in order to prevent sore nipples. However, other doctors and the La Leche League feel this isn't necessary if the baby is nursing properly. Since it may take two or three minutes for the milk to let down, a baby should be allowed at first to nurse about ten minutes on each breast. Then, the time can be lengthened to ten minutes on the first breast and twenty minutes on the second. A full feeding usually takes about a half hour.

If your baby starts to lose interest before a feeding is finished, you may perk up his appetite by switching back and forth between breasts. However, some babies become real pros and can efficiently take in enough milk with only five minutes of nursing per breast.

HOW MUCH MILK

It's natural for a new mother to wonder "Is my baby getting enough milk?" After all, there's no way you can measure the ounces as the baby nurses. According to the La Leche League, here are the signs that should reassure you:

- Your baby has six to eight really wet diapers per day and is receiving nothing but breast milk . . . no supplemental bottles of water. (Disposable diapers often do not feel as wet as cloth diapers.)
- Your baby is gaining weight at an average of four to seven ounces a week. Remember that it's normal for breastfed babies to lose a little weight in the first week. Some babies might take three or four weeks to regain their birth weight.
- Your baby appears healthy, with good color and resilient skin (not loose). He's also alert and active with good muscle tone.

CARING FOR YOUR BREASTS

Another advantage of breastfeeding is that you don't have to boil the nipples . . . thank goodness! While no one would go that far, some women feel that it's necessary to thoroughly wash their breasts with soap and water before each feeding. Not only is this unnecessary (an anti-bacterial substance is secreted with breast milk), but these frequent washings can cause the nipples to dry and crack . . . then feedings really can be painful! You can gently wipe your breasts with a damp washcloth or cotton balls after a feeding, but one daily washing with plain water is sufficient.

To prevent cracking and soreness, the best treatment is leave your nipples exposed to the air after each feeding until they are completely dry. A nursing bra makes it easy to leave the flaps down and it provides good support but make sure it isn't too tight. Cream on the breast is usually not necessary and the process of removing it before a feeding can be tough on the nipples. If your doctor recommends an ointment, like A & D, apply it lightly so it has time to be absorbed before the next feeding—some babies are fussy about flavored milk!

It's common for breasts to become engorged two to four days after delivery or if a feeding is missed. The breasts feel hard, heavy and may be painful. Your baby may also have difficulty latching on properly. You can get relief by expressing milk, or massaging the breasts while taking a warm shower. During nursing, you can help your baby empty your breasts more completely by massaging the breast in a circular motion. This is important in preventing mastitis or infections in the breast. If an area becomes sore, warm or there's redness, call your doctor right away.

HAND-EXPRESSING MILK

It may take a little practice, but it's important for a nursing mother to be able to express some milk by hand, especially if the breast is so engorged that the baby can't latch on properly. The basic technique is really quite easy:

1. Cup your breast in your hand with your thumb above, fingers below, supporting the breast.
2. Push back toward the chest wall while squeezing your thumb and fingers together rhythmically just behind the areola. Do not slide your fingers along the skin.
3. Rotate your hand around the breast in order to reach all the milk ducts, it should take about three to five minutes. If you are expressing to relieve engorgement before a feeding, only do it until the areola is soft enough for your baby to grasp.
4. Switch to the other breast and repeat.

If you want to save the milk for a later feeding, make sure your hands are clean and the milk is expressed into a sterile plastic container. (Plastic is better than glass containers for collection and feeding since the cells in breast milk that protect against infection tend to cling to the sides of glass jars—they never get to your baby.) The milk should then be refrigerated immediately.

Once your baby becomes an old pro at breastfeeding, usually by three or four weeks, an occasional bottle isn't likely to confuse him. It will certainly give you a well-deserved chance to catch up on sleep or have an afternoon off. Also, this is the time fathers or older siblings can get in on the fun of feeding the baby. A bottle has the best chance of being accepted if it's given by someone other than the mother. Why should a baby settle for a bottle when the real thing is only inches away!

USING A BREAST PUMP

Although some women are able manually to express enough milk, others find it easier to use one of the large variety of breast pumps—some are hand operated, others use batteries and a few are electrical (this type is most expensive, but can often be rented). If you're going back to work and plan to continue breastfeeding, you'll probably need to use a pump. La Leche League describes the pros and cons of different types in their free "Breast Pump Flyer" and several pumps can be purchased through the organization. Here are some tips on using any breast pump:

- Follow the manufacturer's directions carefully.
- Moisten your breast to improve suction before applying the breast shield.
- Go easy at first and use the lowest setting or the least amount of suction to get started. It is possible to damage sensitive breast tissue, so stop at the first sign of discomfort. If necessary, switch to a different brand or type of pump.

JOAN: **In the first week after delivery, a friend of mine used an electric pump so strongly it caused really painful uterine contractions and bleeding. She had to go back into the hospital for a D & C.**

- Pumping in a quiet relaxed setting and looking at your baby or his picture will usually help the milk to flow more smoothly.

STORING BREAST MILK

If you must be separated from your baby for anytime, or you return to work, you can express milk regularly. That way you can continue breastfeeding and your baby can benefit from all the advantages of breast milk. Fortunately, it can be stored quite well— up to forty-eight hours in the refrigerator, two weeks in the freezer compartment of a refrigerator or up to two years in a separate freezer at zero degrees Fahrenheit. Remember to label each batch of milk with the date and time. Here are some other tips:

- After expressing your milk into a sterile plastic container, transfer it into sterilized baby bottles or plastic nurser bags.
- Use a separate sterile container to refrigerate the milk each time you express. These cooled batches can then be combined for a feeding or freezing.
- Freeze the milk in small amounts, from two to four ounces, so there's less chance of waste. Allow room for expansion.
- When freezing in plastic nurser bags, use them double to avoid tearing. Squeeze out the air, roll down to one inch above the milk and fasten well. Store the bags in a box or bag designed for long-term freezer storage.
- Once breast milk is defrosted, never refreeze it.
- Refrigerated or thawed breast milk will separate, so shake it gently before giving it to your baby.

For instructions on temperature and giving your baby a bottle, look up those areas in the section on FORMULA FEEDING YOUR BABY (pp. 81–90).

PRODUCING NUTRITIOUS BREAST MILK

The quantity and quality of your breast milk depends on your eating a balanced diet of healthy foods. It's basically the same requirements as when you were pregnant. This is not the time for crash diets! Here are daily recommendations:

- Five servings of the milk group—milk, cheese, yogurt, etc.—for calcium.
- Four servings of protein foods. If you are a vegetarian, you must combine foods carefully so you are eating complete protein.
- Four or more servings of vegetables and fruits, including at least one citrus fruit (vitamin C); and at least one serving of a yellow or green vegetable or fruit (vitamin A).
- Four servings of whole grain or enriched breads or cereals.
- To produce enough milk, your total fluid intake should be two to three quarts of milk, juice or water, not soda which just fills you up with empty calories and often contains caffeine.

- Continue taking your prenatal vitamin and mineral supplement, but don't consider it as a substitute for a good diet. Also, don't take large amounts of other supplements—they can be toxic to your baby.
- If you are a strict vegetarian (no milk or eggs), you will produce milk that is deficient in vitamin B12 and you should take supplements under your doctor's direction.

JOAN: And here's the advice that was really good news to me! You're supposed to splurge with an extra 500 calories daily for the first couple months, then increase it to 800 calories. That means you can eat 2,100 to 2,900 calories a day without gaining weight. They'll be used up in producing milk. Just be sure they come from healthful, high-nutrition foods, not junk foods.

SAFE BREAST MILK

You must also be aware that your breast milk will reflect many other things besides the nutrients in your diet. Almost every drug that you take, prescription or over-the-counter, will transfer into your milk. So you must check with your doctor before taking any medication. Here are some other things to watch out for:

Alcohol. Research is being done on the effects of alcohol and the general opinion is that a moderate amount—one drink, or glass of wine or beer, a day—is harmless to an infant. Keep in mind that the concentration of alcohol in your milk will be nearly as much as the concentration in your blood.

Caffeine. This is present in coffee, tea, chocolate and many soft drinks. Its level is the same in breast milk as in the mother's system and may accumulate in the baby's blood. There is controversy over what level is harmful to an infant, so it's best to keep your caffeine intake as low as possible.

Nicotine. Although the amount of nicotine in the breast milk of moderate smokers has not been shown to be harmful to infants, nicotine can reduce the amount of milk production. So the recommendation is—don't smoke!

Environmental Contaminents.   There has been concern about the levels of the chemical PCB and insecticides in breast milk. The American Academy of Pediatrics states that most women have little to fear. If you have worked directly with toxic chemicals or have eaten large amounts of fish taken from contaminated waters or live in areas where there are continuously high levels of pollutants, you can have your breast milk tested.

THE FATHER'S ROLE IN BREASTFEEDING

There's obviously no way that a father can be directly involved when an infant is breastfed, so there's no reason for him to feel guilty about the amount of the mother's time that's required for feeding. And even though it's also normal for a father to feel a little left out of this close relationship between the mother and their baby, there's no need to. During these early weeks, when so much of the mother's energy is concentrated on nursing, the father's support and help is really necessary.

In the first place, it's so important to recognize all the time and energy a new mother spends with a baby and to give her loving reassurance and understanding. Every day I tell Joan she's doing a great job and I thank her for taking such good care of Sarah. But besides words, there are lots of tangible ways for a father to help out when he's home. For instance, when Sarah cries for a feeding, I bring her to Joan. Then when she's finished nursing, I take over the job of burping her . . . an art that I'm proud of. And even after she burps, I spend a lot of time just cuddling and talking to her. Think of it this way—a baby needs to be fed with lots more than just milk. Babies need hugs, kisses, words, even music and fathers are just as capable of giving these as mothers. When you do enough little things, it really adds up, both for the baby and the father.

Of course there can be a fine line between encouraging a father to be involved (that includes not being critical of the way he burps or bathes the baby) and putting on more demands than he can handle. I don't mind changing the baby, but I know some men who just can't stand the sight of a soiled diaper. Also, since the father often has to work during the day, it's unrealistic to expect him to get up every couple hours to help with feedings. On the other hand, giving an occasional supplemental bottle can allow the mother a few hours of well-needed uninterrupted sleep. The most important thing is for both parents to communicate to each other how they feel and to work out the best way to make these first few weeks as relaxed as possible. It's a very special time and it should be enjoyed.

FORMULA-FEEDING YOUR BABY

There's no question that breast milk is the ideal food for an infant's first year. But what if you can't breastfeed your baby for some medical reason? Or you have strong feelings against breast-feeding? Or you have been nursing your baby and for one reason or another, decide to stop? Well, there's no reason to feel guilty!

Commercial infant formulas are designed to be as close as possible to the nutritional composition of breast milk. All infant formulas comply with the amounts of nutrients as recommended by the Committee on Nutrition of the American Academy of Pediatrics. The chart on pages 82–83 is excerpted from the Academy's "Guidelines for Perinatal Care."

Types of Formula

Most commercial formulas are prepared from modified cow's milk. If a baby has an adverse reaction to milk (see When "Something" Doesn't Agree), there are soy-based or other specialized formulas available. However, these formulas should NOT be routinely given unless your baby's doctor recommends them. The same goes for the "iron" or "low-iron fortified" formulas. Your doctor should decide which is best for your baby.

Formulas also come in various forms:

- "Ready-to-feed" is obviously the easiest to use, but it is also the most expensive. It's available in eight or thirty-two fluid ounce cans, and four, six and eight fluid ounce glass bottles—all you need to do is screw on a nipple. They're really convenient when you're traveling.

Source and Composition of Infant Formulas

Formula/milk	Calories/oz	PROTEIN		FAT		CARBOHYDRATE		SODIUM (mEq/liter)	POTASSIUM (mEq/liter)	Phosphorus (mg/dl)	Calcium (mg/dl)
		Source	g/dl	Source	g/dl	Source	g/dl				
Feeding at Infancy											
Human milk	20	Human milk	1.0–1.2	Human milk	4.5	Lactose	7.0	7	13	16	34
Enfamil	20	Skim milk	1.5	Soy oil, coconut oil	3.7	Lactose	7.0	12	18	46	55
Isomil	20	Soy protein isolate with L-methionine	2.0	Soy oil, coconut oil	3.6	Corn syrup, sucrose	6.8	13	18	50	70
Lofenalac	20	Casein hydrolysate	2.2	Corn oil	2.7	Corn syrup solids, tapioca starch	8.7	14	17	47	63
Nursoy	20	Soy isolate with L-methionine	2.1	Oleo, coconut oil, plain soy	3.6	Sucrose	6.9	8	18	42	60

82

		Protein source	Protein	Fat source	Fat	Carbohydrate source	CHO				
Nutramigen	20	Casein hydrolysate	2.2	Corn oil	2.6	Sucrose, tapioca starch	8.8	14	17	47	63
Portagen	20	Casein	2.4	MCT, corn oil	3.2	Corn syrup solids, sucrose, lactose	7.8	14	22	47	63
Prosobee	20	Soy protein isolate with L-methionine	2.0	Soy oil, coconut oil	3.6	Corn syrup solids	6.9	12	17	47	60
Similac	20	Skim milk	1.6	Coconut oil, soy oil	3.6	Lactose	7.2	11	20	39	51
SMA	20	Whey, casein	1.5	Oleo, coconut oil, safflower oil, soy oil	3.5	Lactose	7.2	6	14	33	44
Soyalac	20	Soybean solids	2.1	Soy oil	3.7	Sucrose, corn syrup solids	6.6	13	19	50	60
Cow's milk	20	Cow's milk	3.3	Cow's milk	3.7	Lactose	4.8	25	35	95	124

- "Concentrated liquid" is sold in thirteen ounce cans and must be diluted with water.
- "Concentrated powder" must also be diluted with water and is available in sixteen ounce cans or single-feeding packets. The advantage of this form is that it's the lightest to carry home and takes up less storage room.

Purchasing and Storage

All infant formula containers carry "use by" or "use before" dates to ensure that the contents are fresh and of high-quality. Beyond these expiration dates, some vitamin levels decrease and there may be discoloration or separation of fat. Do not buy formula that is past the expiration date, or store it so long at home that it becomes outdated.

- Keep unopened formula in a cool, dry place. Warm temperatures can affect quality.
- Opened cans of liquid formula should be tightly covered and kept in the refrigerator no more than forty-eight hours.
- Formula that has been prepared from powder or concentrate and sterilized (see Sterilization) can be stored in the refrigerator up to forty-eight hours.
- Freezing formula is not recommended since it may cause physical separation.
- DO NOT keep any formula left over from a feeding— microorganisms have multiplied and could cause intestinal infections. If your baby rarely finishes her bottle, you're probably giving too much. (See How Much Formula.)

Bottles and Nipples

There is quite a selection of bottles and nipples and each have their advantages. You have to decide what's best for you and your baby. Here are some points to consider:

- The disposable plastic liners are sterile and save bottle washing, but they are more expensive to use.
- The rigid bottles, either plastic or glass, can be warmed in a microwave.
- The clear bottles allow light to enter, and that can reduce the amount of the vitamin riboflavin in the formula. The colored ones screen out much of the light.
- The orthodontic-type nipples are designed to simulate a mother's nipples, so if you're giving a supplemental bottle or you're weaning your baby, she might adapt more easily to this type of nipple.

Preparing Formula

If you're using the "ready-to-feed" formula, all you have to do is wash off the top of the can, give it a shake, and open it with a *clean* can opener (keep one just for formulas), and pour it into the bottle.

If you're using concentrated liquid or powder formula, you must dilute it with water that has been boiled for five minutes. When you're mixing each bottle just before a feeding, you can save time if you boil all the water you need for the day and keep it in the refrigerator.

The most important thing to remember when using a concentrate is to dilute it *exactly* according to the directions—it is usually EQUAL amounts of formula and water. For example, if you use ten ounces of formula, dilute it with 10 ounces of water.

- DO NOT ADD MORE FORMULA because you think your baby will be getting more nutrition. The higher concentration will just put more strain on his digestive system and could result in dehydration, kidney stones and other serious problems.
- DO NOT ADD MORE WATER because you are trying to save money or you feel your baby is overweight. Your baby needs the exact concentration of nutrients in each bottle of formula.

Sterilization

In the past, sterilization was important when a day's supply of formula was prepared from cow's milk or evaporated milk. It slowed down the growth of bacteria that caused intestinal infections. Now, commercial infant formula is already sterilized. Most doctors don't require sterilization of the bottles or nipples if the formula is prepared less than three hours before each feeding. Of course, everything, including your hands, should be washed thoroughly! (Just be sure to rinse all the soap from the bottles and nipples. A residue can cause diarrhea.)

Many parents find it more convenient to prepare enough formula for at least a full day's feeding—at two A.M. it's a real blessing! In this case, you must sterilize all the preparation equipment you use (including the can opener), and the bottles (unless disposables) and the nipples. You do this by boiling everything for twenty minutes. Then fill the sterile bottles with prepared formula and refrigerate.

JOAN: **Our pediatrician, Dr. Brown, showed me this alternative method that he says many parents have found is faster and more convenient. It's called "terminal sterilization."**

1.   **Line up the bottles (use only the rigid type).**
2.   **Fill with formula and tap water according to directions.**
3.   **Invert the nipples and put the caps on loosely.**
4.   **Place the bottles upright in a large pot with three inches of water. A "sterilizer" pot, containing racks is easiest, if you can find one.**
5.   **Cover the pot and boil for twenty-five minutes.**
6.   **Tighten the caps and refrigerate.**

How Much Formula?

When an infant is breastfed, there is no easy way of knowing how much milk is taken at any feeding. When the baby finishes nursing and seems satisfied, the mother assumes an adequate amount of milk has been consumed. However, when you are feeding your baby with a bottle that is marked with ounce measurements, you can know exactly how much the baby takes in—try not to look!

Unfortunately, the tendency is to encourage a baby to finish a bottle "to the last drop." What you're really doing is establishing the undesirable habit of overfeeding which can lead to overweight. Studies have shown that formula-fed infants tend to gain more weight than breastfed infants, probably due to overfeeding. Remember, your baby doesn't have to be fat to be well-nourished!

If your baby wisely resists your bottle-pushing, the result can be a lot of tension associated with feedings and that's just the opposite of the relaxed atmosphere that's so beneficial. So respect your baby's wishes! A bottle-fed infant, just as a breastfed infant, when given a free choice, will usually consume the right amount for optimum growth and development. His needs may vary with periodic growth spurts and his individual level of activity. Some infants are placid and some are constantly moving. The desire for food may also vary from day to day, just as with older children and adults.

So keep all this mind as you look at the following chart that lists recommended daily calories and ounces of formula. It's based on the requirements of the average healthy infant and can be useful as a guide to know how much formula to prepare each day. The total amount can generally be divided into six to eight feedings.

Recommended Amounts of Formula per 24 Hours

BABY'S WEIGHT	CALORIES*	FORMULA**
6 pounds	312	16 ounces
7	364	18
8	416	21
9	468	23
10	520	26
11	572	29
12	624	31
13	672	34
14	672	34

* Calories are calculated from the U.S. 1980 Recommended Dietary Allowances for average infants from birth to 6 months. Individual activity levels may change requirements.

** Most formulas contain 20 calories per ounce.

Temperature of Formula

There is nothing more frustrating than listening to your baby cry while you wait for a bottle to warm. Or you've gotten it too hot and now you're trying to cool it down. And it's all so unnecessary! There is no reason, nutritional or psychological, that you can't give your baby formula that is room temperature or even cold. If you're chilled by the thought of cold milk in her warm tummy, don't worry. By the time the formula is halfway down the baby's throat, it's been warmed by her own body heat.

Unwarmed bottles are certainly more convenient, especially at night or when you're traveling. They can also be healthier. If you warm formula in anticipation of a feeding and your baby decides to snooze a little longer, it can give bacteria a chance to multiply. What's important is to be consistent. Don't serve warm formula one day and cold the next, or your baby might reject what's unfamiliar.

*WARNING! You should never use a microwave to heat formula in the disposable plastic nursers. Since heated air expands, the plastic bags can explode and scald your baby.

You can use a microwave oven to heat formula in rigid bottles, but be careful.

- Leave the tops off.
- Use a low setting.
- Shake to distribute the heat.
- Always test the temperature before feeding your baby. Shake a little on the inside of your wrist—it should feel barely warm.

Of course, the last two steps should be followed no matter how you warm a bottle!

Giving The Bottle

This is really the easy part! But don't be tempted to prop the bottle in the baby's mouth—it may cause choking. Also, formula-fed babies need the same close contact during feedings as breastfed babies. The advantage is that now the father, the grandparents and

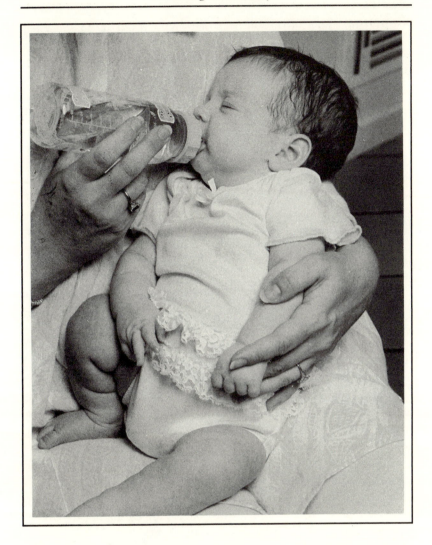

older siblings can also share in the pleasure of feeding the baby. Just relax in a comfortable chair, hold the baby in your lap and support his head in the bend of your arm. A small pillow can make the position more comfortable.

Here are some other tips:

- The baby's head and shoulders should be slightly raised. If he's flat on his back, some formula might be forced into the inner ear canals and that could result in an inner ear infection.

- Always tilt the bottle so the neck is filled with formula. This helps to keep the baby from swallowing air.
- If the nipple collapses, loosen the cap to let some air into the bottle. Then tighten it and continue feeding.
- When the baby is halfway through the feeding, stop and give him a chance to burp. (See Burping Your Baby, p. 91.)

Demand or Schedule Feeding

Just as with breastfed babies, the best schedule for a formula-fed baby is no schedule . . . babies usually prefer small frequent feedings. However, if this is not practical for some reason—you're working, you have older children who have their own demands or you're the type of person who likes to be able to plan your day— you can try to encourage your baby to settle down to some kind of schedule. And, since formula is digested more slowly than breast milk, your baby is likely to go longer between feedings.

The usual recommendation for a daytime schedule is a minimum of three hours between feedings and a maximum of four hours. If your baby gets in the habit of longer naps during the day, he may get up more frequently at night! Keep in mind, though, that babies are individuals from the minute they're born—some will adapt more easily to a schedule than others. If you have a baby who resists, a schedule might be more trouble than it's worth. It may be comforting to know that by three months, most babies are eating at predictable intervals and even sleeping through the night!

Now, if your baby cries well before a scheduled feeding, or is on demand feeding and seems to be too demanding, consider this—babies don't always cry because they're hungry! (See Chapter 10 . . . Your Baby's Crying.) For example, your baby may be wet, uncomfortable or just plain lonely. Remember, you can't spoil your baby with cuddling. So check out everything before you rush to give a bottle. Formula-fed babies don't usually require extra water, but if it's a hot day or he's ill, you can try offering some water (boiled for twenty minutes). He may just be thirsty.

BURPING YOUR BABY

Whether your baby nurses at your breast or from a bottle, chances are he'll also swallow some air. How much depends on how good a grip he has on the nipple—the looser the grip, the more air. This can give a baby a false sense of being full, so he falls asleep before he's really finished and then wakes up in an hour or so . . . hungry again!

If your baby is an air swallower, you should give him a chance to burp in the middle of a feeding and try again at the end. Going to sleep with trapped air in the tummy can cause discomfort as it makes its way through the intestines. Here are the most effective positions for producing a burp:

1. Hold your baby upright, with his chin resting on your shoulder.

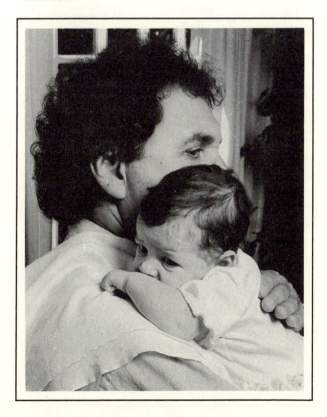

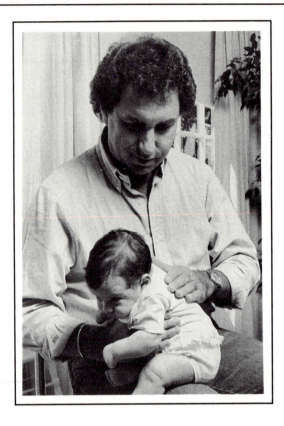

2. Sit him up in your lap, lean him forward against your arm and support his chin with your hand.
3. Lay him stomach-down across your lap with his head turned sideways.

Whatever position you try, make sure his mouth and nose are in the clear and then gently rub or pat his back. You don't have to thump! Give him a minute or so, and if nothing happens, don't worry . . . some babies just don't need to burp.

You should also have a diaper on your shoulder or in your lap to catch any milk that's brought up with the burped air. If your baby doesn't really burp, but tends to spit up sometime in the future (catching people unprepared) try laying him down on his tummy for a while. Recent studies have shown this works better than sitting a baby up in an infant seat.

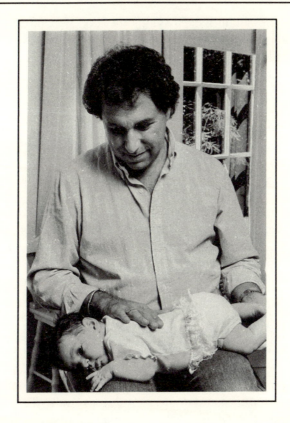

WHEN "SOMETHING" DOESN'T AGREE

When your normally happy baby has abdominal pain, diarrhea or vomits after a feeding, it could mean that he's ill. However, if it continues, it could be caused by the milk he's drinking. Babies can react badly to milk for several reasons.

The least likely problem during the first year is a rare congenital inability to digest the lactose in milk. Usually, babies are born with the lactase enzyme that is essential in breaking down lactose. Then, after the first year or two, the enzyme starts to decline. This is most common among children of American Indian, African, Mexican, Asian, Middle Eastern and Jewish descent. This intolerance to lactose is not the same as being allergic to milk.

Allergy or hypersensitivity to the protein in cow's milk is more common, affecting an estimated twelve percent of infants and young children. Some infants show symptoms soon after birth. For others it may take weeks or months before symptoms show up. The tendency to allergies does seem to be inherited, so check out your family history. An allergy to cow's milk protein may also produce a variety of symptoms:

vomiting	wheezing
diarrhea	canker sores
cramps and gas	eczema
hives	chronic runny nose

Do be alert to the persistence of any of these symptoms, especially after feedings, and bring them to your doctor's attention. Remember, any diagnosis of milk allergy or lactose intolerance should be made by your baby's doctor! If your baby is formula-fed, the doctor will probably recommend switching to a soy-based formula. They are designed to supply the same nutrients as cow's milk formulas. For those infants who are also sensitive to soybean milk there are special elemental formulas in which the protein is already partially broken down . . . these formulas must be prescribed by a doctor.

The protein in breast milk is different from cow's milk and it's very rare for a baby to be allergic to breast milk. This is another good reason to nurse your baby, especially if allergies seem to run in the family. However, a breastfed infant may still show some symptoms. This can be caused by the mother drinking large amounts of cow's milk. The offending proteins do enter the mother's milk. If you suspect this might be the cause, try eliminating milk from your diet for a week or so and see what happens. If it is the milk, you can try substituting yogurt or cheese.

However, milk may not be the culprit. Your baby may be reacting to other foods you are eating. The ones most likely to cause allergies are:

egg whites	citrus fruits
berries	tomatoes
fish	wheat
shellfish	corn
nuts	chocolate

Members of the cabbage family can also cause gasiness. If you've been eating lots of any of these foods, try eliminating them (one at a time) for a few days. In case your baby does show a sensitivity to a food during breastfeeding, make a note to skip that food when you start giving your baby solids.

SUPPLEMENTS

The American Academy of Pediatrics advises that breast milk (from a well-nourished mother) or formula will supply enough of most of the vitamins and minerals your newborn needs—at least for the first four to six months. You should NEVER give your baby supplements unless they are prescribed by your baby's doctor. There is more danger of toxicity from the misuse of vitamin and mineral supplements than there is of a deficiency. Here are the supplements your doctor may recommend:

- *Fluoride* may be given if you are breastfeeding (it does not enter breast milk); you are using only ready-to-feed formula; or you are using concentrated formula and your water supply contains less than 0.3 parts per million of fluoride. The baby's teeth are being formed during these first months and fluoride may help protect them against later cavities. Fluoride supplements should not exceed 0.25 mg daily or tooth discoloration may occur.
- *Vitamin D* may be given to breastfed babies (usually after three months) if they don't get much exposure to sunlight or they are dark-skinned.

NOTE: Iron is NOT usually recommended during the early months. Healthy full-term babies are born with enough iron to last four to six months.

*WARNING: Never give your baby more than the recommended amount of a supplement. It can be dangerous!

CHAPTER 7
YOUR BABY'S BOTTOM

THE INEVITABLE RESULT OF feeding your baby is the elimination of urine and stool. And it's common for new parents to worry almost as much about what comes out as what goes in. To relieve that concern, you'll find out in this chapter everything you need to know about the contents of your baby's diapers!

> JOAN: **Before our first baby was born, it never occurred to me that I would spend so much time looking at and**

worrying over "poopie" diapers. But in the first few weeks, that's what concerned me the most! I was confused about the change in color and it seemed to me the baby always had diarrhea. It took countless calls and questions before my pediatrician convinced me these were normal bowel movements for a breastfed baby.

THE DIFFERENT TYPES OF STOOLS

The color and consistency of your baby's stools can vary considerably. In the first few days after birth, the newborn will pass a greenish-black sticky substance called meconium. This is made up of swallowed amniotic fluid and excess red blood cells that are no longer needed. If you are breastfeeding, the colostrum will have a laxative effect and help your baby get rid of the meconium more quickly. Also, don't panic if you notice some blood in these stools. It's usually caused by tiny amounts of blood from the placenta or cervix getting into the amniotic fluid that your baby swallowed. Your doctor can easily verify this through a simple blood test.

The next stools your baby will produce are not so dark and look rather like bird seed. These are called transitional. After the first week or two, your baby's stools will assume their regular color and consistency . . . both of which depend on what he's eating.

Breastfed babies have stools that are usually a yellowish color with a very liquid, mustard-like consistency. At first, they may only appear as a stain on the diaper. The odor is also quite inoffensive (another advantage of breastfeeding)! **Formula-fed** babies have stronger smelling, firmer, darker stools, especially if the formula contains added iron. Soy-based formulas produce stools that are gray-green and look like concentrated split pea soup.

Finally, whether your baby is breastfed or formula-fed, he may occasionally produce a greenish stool—don't worry! This only means the food passed through his system so quickly not all the bile was absorbed.

Frequency

Once again, remember that your baby is an individual and that applies to how often he has a bowel movement. Some babies stool after every feeding, others go daily and some wait two to three days between stools—it's all normal. You'll soon become familiar with your baby's pattern, though it may still vary from week to week. In general, breastfed babies will have more frequent stools than babies who are fed formula.

But if there's so much variation in frequency, how can you recognize when your baby really is constipated or has diarrhea? Actually, constipation is more related to consistency than frequency. Babies also normally turn red, make noises and strain when they have bowel movements! However, if your baby has a lot of difficulty passing stools that are hard, dry and look like pebbles, he is probably constipated. When this happens three or four times in a row, call your doctor. Don't give laxatives or suppositories unless advised to.

Diarrhea is also diagnosed by the consistency of your baby's stools—they are watery, with small flecks, and have a powerful smell! Diarrhea can be caused by an upper respiratory infection; a reaction to an antibiotic; an intestinal infection; or an allergy to some food, such as cow's milk (even if you are breastfeeding, proteins from the milk you drink will be in your breast milk). If diarrhea continues, your baby runs the risk of becoming dehydrated (he's eliminating more water and salts than he's taking in) so call your doctor!

> JOAN: **I've found it's really useful, at least for the first few weeks, to use a daily diary and keep a record of the baby's bowel movements. That way I can easily spot when anything's out of the ordinary and when I call the doctor, he usually wants to know about the last few bowel movements. In the same diary I also make a note of each feeding, another thing doctors often ask about.**

URINATION

Newborn babies usually urinate during the first twenty-four hours and this first urine is normally rather dark and murky due to high concentration of some crystals and proteins. When your baby begins eating well, she should produce at least six to eight wet diapers a day. If you're caught off guard while diapering (babies urinate frequently), you'll notice the urine has a light yellow color.

In the first week or two after birth, however, the urine may be slightly pink. Don't assume it's blood and panic! This is usually caused by a temporary high concentration of a certain amino acid, but your doctor should still check the urine, so save the diaper to bring to the office. In general, if you notice any variation in the color or frequency of urination, bring it to your doctor's attention.

DIAPER RASH

A common result of the baby's bottom coming into frequent contact with stool and urine is diaper rash. It begins as a slight redness, and left untreated the rash can develop into open sores that may become infected. But there's no need for things to go that far.

JOAN: Each of our babies has suffered from the inevitable diaper rash, but Dr. Brown alleviated any guilt by pointing out that "If adults wore diapers they would get diaper rash." His advice for keeping it under control is to expose the area to fresh air as often as possible, especially if the rash has reached the open sore stage. I would let the baby nap on her tummy on a cloth diaper on top of a square of waterproof flannel sheeting. A baby's tush is cute to look at even if it is a little red! Or I would pin the diaper to the front and back of the undershirt, leaving the sides open. Of course, if the air can get in, things can also leak out—but it's worth it to your baby.

If you need a little more protection, and your baby wears plastic pants, get some scissors and snip the elastic around the legs. The same goes for disposable diapers with elastic. They can be too efficient at keeping moisture in and the air out. You should never use plastic pants over a disposable diaper.

However, there are times when your baby needs to wear a really secure diaper, like going out or when visitors come to admire and play with him. You can help protect your baby's bottom by applying a thin coating of a protective cream like A & D ointment or zinc oxide, but first make sure the area is completely dry. By the way, since these creams resist moisture, they are really tough to remove during a diaper change. Dr. Brown's trick is to use baby oil.

You should check with your doctor before using any medication on the rash. Some creams, like hydrocortisone, should not be used on open sores since they can get into the bloodstream. Other medication can damage the skin if used for any length of time. Also, don't use cornstarch. It allows the growth of yeast-like organisms.

If the rash persists, it may be caused by a yeast infection called thrush (see p. 51) which should be treated by your doctor. This type of rash starts with red bumpy patches, usually in the creases, and spreads outward. Tiny blisters form and then break, leaving the skin raw.

Of course the best way to prevent diaper rash is to change your baby's diapers frequently and clean the area thoroughly. In case it's caused by an allergy, you might try changing the brand of disposables and using the unscented type. Or, if your baby wears cloth diapers, don't use a fabric softener, change the type of detergent and make sure they are thoroughly rinsed, adding a little vinegar to the final rinse helps. But if after everything, a rash still appears, don't feel guilty. Your baby may just have very sensitive skin!

THE ART OF DIAPERING

Since you can spend almost as much time diapering your baby as feeding her, here is an easy, step-by-step guide to the fine art of diapering:

1. RULE #1: KEEP ONE HAND ON OR NEAR THE BABY ALL THE TIME SHE IS ON THE CHANGING TABLE! Don't depend on restraining straps or the fact that she

doesn't yet know how to roll over. There's always going to be that first time!

2. Before you put the baby on the changing table, have everything within easy reach, but where she can't knock them over. You'll need plain water, baby oil, cotton balls, a washcloth, protective cream, towels and diapers. The premoistened towelettes are convenient, but more expensive.
   - Take the tops off any bottles or jars and have the fresh diaper ready to go. If you're using a cloth diaper, here's how to fold it:

3. Place your baby on the table, secure the safety snap and remove the diaper, but be prepared! Babies urinate frequently anyway, so the odds aren't in your favor, and the change in temperature is often all your baby needs. Little boys can produce a stream twelve to eighteen inches high, but at least they usually give warning with an erection. Wait a few seconds after opening the diaper before removing it, or have a diaper ready to throw over the area.

4. Then wipe off any stool and urine with cotton balls soaked in lukewarm water (or use baby oil first to remove protective cream). You can also use the premoistened towelettes, but if your baby has a rash, avoid the ones that contain alcohol. Soap isn't usually necessary, and it can dry out the skin which promotes diaper rash.
   - Girls should be cleaned "front to back" to prevent stool from causing vaginal or urinary tract infections.

- Clean and rinse all areas thoroughly. This helps prevent diaper rash. You can even dip your baby's bottom in a bowl of lukewarm water.
- If your little boy is uncircumcised, remember the American Academy of Pediatrics' warning—DO NOT TRY TO RETRACT THE FORESKIN in order to clean under it. This might cause tearing that could produce scar tissue and prevent normal separation.
- If he has been circumcised, follow your doctor's instructions on caring for the wound.

5. Next, it's very important to completely dry the area, including all the creases. Pat gently with a towel. If your baby has a sore rash, fan it dry or use a hair dryer on a warm setting. Just be sure to test it first on your hand. Don't use a heat or sun lamp!

6. You can then apply a thin layer of a protective cream. If there's no rash, petroleum jelly is adequate. Of course, if you're going to leave the diaper off for a while, don't use any cream. You want the air to be able to reach the skin.
   - If the baby has a heat rash, you can use powder instead of cream, but it should contain an anti-fungal ingredient. Don't use cornstarch around the diaper area. In general, powders may smell nice, but they aren't necessary.

7. Finally, you're ready to put on a fresh diaper. The disposables with the adhesive tabs are really easy. If you're using cloth diapers, fasten them with diaper pins, not plain safety pins that can open easily. You can stick the pins in a bar of soap to make them slide through the cloth smoothly.

CHAPTER 8
WHEN TO CALL YOUR BABY'S DOCTOR

ONCE THE BABY IS brought home, it's only natural for parents, especially first-timers, to worry whenever "something" just doesn't seem "right." First of all, it helps to be well-informed! In Chapter 5 . . . YOUR BABY FROM HEAD TO TOE, you've seen what's normal in newborns, and some of the problems. There are also some excellent children's medical guides that cover every symptom and illness in children of all ages, and it's a good idea to have one at home.

JOAN: **Dr. Brown wrote a very useful guide to** *How, When and Why to Call Your Child's Doctor* **even before he became our pediatrician, so I knew I wasn't the only paranoid parent who called every time the baby sneezed. Eventually, through experience, lots of reading and Dr. Brown's patient explanations, I did become less anxious.**

Since, it's your doctor that you'll turn to most for advice, reassurance, diagnosis and treatment, the question that worries many parents is . . . "WHEN should I call the doctor?" They're afraid they might bother him with too many calls and questions. If you feel this way, stop worrying. Remember, that's a part of his chosen profession and you've chosen your particular doctor because of his willingness to answer questions. (See Chapter 1 . . . CHOOSING YOUR BABY'S DOCTOR.) However, it is your responsibility to use common sense and consideration as to the timing of your calls.

If you're asking for routine advice in caring for the baby such as "Is he ready for a tub bath?" or you know it's a minor problem like "What should I do about a rash on his face?" call during the doctor's special call-in hour or call during office hours. Often, the nurse will be able to help you.

If you suspect that your baby may be developing a problem or an illness, "The area around the navel is getting redder" or "He's a little fussy and running a fever of 99.8 degrees," don't wait to see if it gets worse and then have to call in the middle of the night! It's best to call during office hours so you can bring him in if the doctor feels it's necessary. This might save everyone a sleepness night!

When Is It An Emergency?

However, there are times when you should NEVER hesitate to call your doctor, no matter what time of the day or night. If you get the receptionist or answering service, describe the symptoms and say that you need to speak to the doctor right away. Here are the symptoms or conditions that Dr. Brown warns parents to be alert for. They require prompt diagnosis and treatment:

THE FONTANEL (the soft spot) IS TENSE OR BULGING.

When a baby is crying or lying down, it's normal for the fontanel to bulge slightly. However, when a baby is quiet and held upright, the fontanel should be slightly sunken. If it bulges or doesn't give when pressed lightly, there may be excess fluid inside the skull.

THE BABY HAS TURNED BLUE.

It's normal for a newborn's chest to be mottled, or his hands and feet to be bluish. His circulation isn't yet working very efficiently. However, if his nail beds, mouth or torso become blue (cyanotic), it means he isn't getting enough oxygen.

THE BABY'S SKIN COLOR HAS BECOME YELLOWISH.

A slight tinge of yellow around the nose is common in newborns, but if his entire skin has turned yellow, it means he has developed jaundice.

THE BABY IS LIMP, DIFFICULT TO AROUSE OR LISTLESS.

Babies should have good muscle tone, and lots of energy. Newborns usually sleep a lot and sleep soundly; however, when they waken (frequently) for feedings, they're wide awake!

THE BABY HAS HAD A CONVULSION.

During a convulsion, the body stiffens, the arms and legs may twitch and there may be a loss of consciousness. It can be over quickly or last five minutes or more. Afterwards, the baby may be limp, not to mention the parents! Now, when a baby gets really worked up and is screaming his lungs out, you may see that his body is stiff and his arms and legs are jerking. Don't be frightened. His loud crying is the reassurance that it's not a convulsion.

YOUR BABY REFUSES TO EAT THROUGH TWO OR MORE FEEDINGS.

In the first day or so after delivery, your newborn may not show much interest in eating. And that's alright—he doesn't need much food during this time. However, once feedings are established, refusing to eat two or three times in a row must be investigated.

YOUR BABY HAS HAD WATERY DIARRHEA THREE OR FOUR TIMES IN A ROW AND SHOWS SIGNS OF DEHYDRATION.

Remember, it's normal for breastfed babies to have runny stools. Diarrhea means that the baby is eliminating stools that are foul smelling, mostly water and contain only small bits of matter. The danger is that young babies can easily become dehydrated if they are losing more water than they are taking in. Some of the signs of severe dehydration are extreme thirst, very sunken fontanel (the soft spot), and little or no urine for several hours.

THERE IS A LARGE AMOUNT OF BLOOD IN THE STOOL OR THE COLOR OF THE STOOL CHANGES TO BLACK.

A few small spots of blood usually come from a small tear in the rectum or an irritated intestine, and are not cause for concern. However, large amounts may indicate internal bleeding.

THERE IS GREEN VOMIT OR PROJECTILE VOMITING (it shoots into the air).

It's common for newborns to vomit small amounts because the valve between the stomach and the esophagus may not yet work properly. It's called reflux. However, vomit that is greenish or that comes shooting out usually indicates an obstruction in the digestive tract.

THE BABY FAILS TO URINATE FOR SEVERAL HOURS OR THERE IS BLOODY URINE.

Young infants urinate frequently, so a dry diaper over several hours may mean there is an obstruction in the urinary tract. Urine that has been normal and then becomes pink or bloody must be checked by the doctor.

THE BABY IS HAVING DIFFICULTY BREATHING.

Since babies breathe through their noses, they can be quite noisy if the nose is stuffed. You can try suctioning the mucous out with a nasal syringe. Just be careful to depress the bulb *before* you insert the syringe into the nose. (See p. 48.)

If this doesn't help and you see the baby gasping and straining with his entire body to take in breaths, it may be due to a more serious problem.

THE BABY HAS A FEVER OVER 101 DEGREES.

A fever is a rise in the body's normal temperature and it is usually a symptom of an illness. What is a "normal" temperature? It is usually 98.6 degrees Fahrenheit (the scale used in the United States), but in some people it can also be slightly lower or slightly higher. A rectal temperature tends to be about a degree higher than one taken orally. Temperatures also tend to vary a few tenths of a degree during the day, being lower in the morning and higher in the evening. The only way to accurately determine if your baby has a fever is to take his temperature with a thermometer. (See TAKING YOUR BABY'S TEMPERATURE.)

Now you may have heard that babies normally run higher fevers than older children, and that's true. So a fever of 101 degrees may not seem high (it's considered low for older children and adults). However, a fever over 101 degrees may be serious in infants under two months. Call your doctor so he can evaluate it in terms of other symptoms.

By the way, the main reason for lowering the temperature is to make the baby more comfortable. Remember, a fever is a symptom of illness, not a cause. Your doctor may advise giving a nonaspirin fever reducer (see GIVING MEDICINE AND VITAMINS). Aspirin should not be used because of its possible link to Reye's Syndrome and viral illnesses.

You may also help reduce the fever, and refresh the baby, by giving a lukewarm bath. It shouldn't be cold or it could chill him. If any relatives believe you can't bathe a sick child, you can tactfully point out that's just an ''old wives' tale''! But you must NEVER give your baby an alcohol rub or put alcohol in the bath water. It may be absorbed into the body and it's dangerous for a baby to breathe alcohol fumes!

YOUR BABY JUST DOESN'T LOOK OR ACT RIGHT.

Finally, even if your baby doesn't show any of the specific symptoms that have been described, you may still feel there is something seriously wrong. Perhaps his cry is different, or he just looks generally sick. You should trust your instincts and call your doctor. Babies are individuals and you're the one who knows *your* baby the best!

TAKING YOUR BABY'S TEMPERATURE

The easiest and most accurate way to take your baby's temperature is rectally. You should use a rectal mercury thermometer (it has a shorter tip) or one of the new digital thermometers that give an instant reading (a big advantage with a squirming baby).

1. If you're using the mercury type, hold it by the non-bulb end and shake it down with a couple quick snaps of your wrist until the mercury line is below the arrow.

2. Lubricating the tip with a little petroleum jelly will make it easier to insert.

3. Place your baby on his stomach or on his back and raise his legs with one hand.

4. Insert the thermometer into the rectum, but be careful that it doesn't go in more than one-half inch. You can support it between your second and third fingers, that way it won't poke the sides of the rectum or slide in further if he squirms.

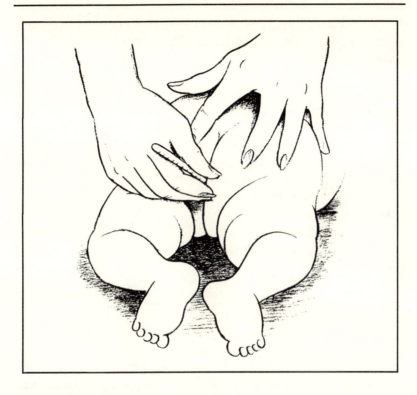

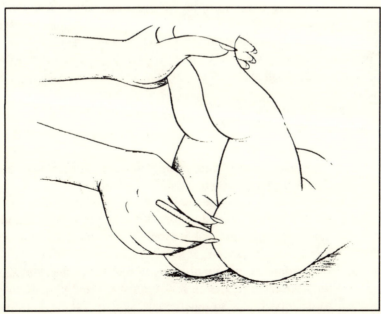

5.   To get a reading, it's only necessary to leave a mercury ther-mometer in for about one minute, not three minutes as many people believe. The digital type only requires a few seconds.

6.   To read a mercury thermometer, hold it by the non-bulb end and rotate it until you see the column of silver-colored mercury. Note the degrees (each short, unnumbered line represents two-tenths of a degree) and write it down, including the date and time. You'll probably be taking your baby's temperature several times and this record will tell your doctor how fast his temperature is going up or down—an important help in diagnosis.

7.   Clean the tip of the thermometer with soap and cold water, or a little alcohol.

WHAT TO TELL YOUR DOCTOR

First of all, unless you are calling during your doctor's special call-in hour (if he has one), you probably won't have your call picked up directly by the doctor. If it's the regular office hours, the nurse or receptionist will usually answer the phone. But if the office is very busy, or it's after hours, an answering service will take over. You should always ask who you are speaking with, then you'll know how much information to give. It's a waste of time to give a detailed explanation of the problem and have the person say "This is just the answering service (or the receptionist)." Even if it's the nurse, it's better to give a brief description and let her ask additional questions.

What information should you leave in your message for the doctor? Here are the basics:

1.   Your name, your child's name and age. This avoids con-fusion if you have more than one child.
2.   A brief description of the immediate problem. You don't need to give a detailed history of the last few days. It adds confusion and the real reason for the call may not get through to the doctor.
3.   Be specific as to how urgent you feel the problem is . . . the answering service or receptionist is usually not trained to do this. If it's an emergency, say so. Likewise if you

need to talk to the doctor as soon as possible, or if you can wait until the doctor next calls in. But, if you're unsure of the seriousness of your baby's condition, it's best to err on the side of caution.

4. Ask how soon the doctor is likely to call back. Knowing this will help alleviate the anxiety of waiting, and since messages can get lost, it gives you an idea of when to call again.

5. Leave a phone number where you can be reached.

Now, when your doctor does call back, be prepared. Have handy any notes you've kept on your baby's symptoms.

> JOAN: **Here's where my daily record of the baby's feedings and bowel movements is useful. I can answer questions about what the pattern normally is, and I know when the last ones were. This is something the doctor usually asks about.**

DATE	TIME	TEMP.
5-4	8:00 AM	99.6
"	10:00	99.7
"	12:00 PM	99.9
"	2:00	100.0
"	2:30	101.0
"	3:00	101.0

You should also have a pad and pencil ready so you can write down your doctor's instructions. When you're anxious, it's easy to forget or confuse things. You should also know the telephone number of your pharmacy in case he wants to call in a prescription. Whatever the problem, here is the basic information that will help your doctor:

1. Give your baby's name and age again to be sure there is no confusion. "I'm calling about my daughter, Lindsay. She's ten days old."
2. Give the most important information. First, describe your baby's immediate symptoms and their severity. "Her temperature half an hour ago was 102 degrees and she's really crying."
3. Then, fill in the background—when the condition started, how fast it's changing or if it has stayed the same. Give the symptoms in the order of their occurrence. "This morning she seemed fussy and didn't nurse very long. Her temperature at ten A.M. was 99.8 degrees."
4. Clearly express what worries you, so the doctor can relieve specific anxieties. For example, "Can a fever like this cause permanent damage?" (The answer is—it's very unlikely.)

JOAN: **Remember, clear communication between you and the doctor is very important. If you feel he hasn't understood the problem, be more specific. If you're not sure of his instructions, don't be afraid to ask him to repeat them (write them down). It's better than having to make another call in the middle of the night.**

GIVING MEDICINE OR VITAMINS

Your doctor carefully prescribes medicine according to your baby's weight, so it's essential to give exactly the right amount. That's why you should never give your baby medicine that was prescribed for an older child. This is one case where "the more, the better'' can cause dangerous side effects. The same goes for over-the-counter drugs and vitamins, especially those that can accumulate in your baby's system. On the other hand, if you give too little, the medicine may not have the desired effect.

Fortunately, most medicines and vitamins intended for babies come with clearly marked droppers. If you have one that doesn't, you should buy a medicine syringe, available in most drugstores. There are also medicine spoons, but these are too difficult to use with young infants. You should never use your kitchen teaspoon to give medicine. It is very likely to hold more or less than a medical teaspoon.

It's also important to pay attention to whether the medicine should be given with a feeding or on an empty stomach. This will help prevent side effects and ensure it works properly. Of course, you should always give medicine, particularly antibiotics, for the length of time advised by the doctor. Don't stop just because the symptoms seem to have gone away. AND NEVER GIVE YOUR BABY MEDICINE THAT WAS LEFTOVER FROM A PREVIOUS ILLNESS UNLESS YOUR DOCTOR SAYS IT'S OKAY!

> JOAN: **Now for the tough part—getting the medicine or vitamins into your baby! Even very young infants seem to have the knack of spitting them out. But don't try slipping them into a bottle of water, formula or breast milk. If your baby doesn't finish the bottle, he will have taken less than he should, and you won't know how much less. Instead, here's a method Dr. Brown showed us that usually works.**
>
> **Place the medicine syringe or dropper in the corner of the baby's cheek and slowly squeeze it in. Don't aim at the back of his throat or squeeze too quickly. He might choke and spit it out.**

Some other tricks that may work—allow the baby to suck on the dropper while you squeeze slowly, or place the measured amount in a nipple and let him suck on it. If he still spits out the medicine, it's safe to repeat the dose, but no more than once. After that, call your doctor for suggestions.

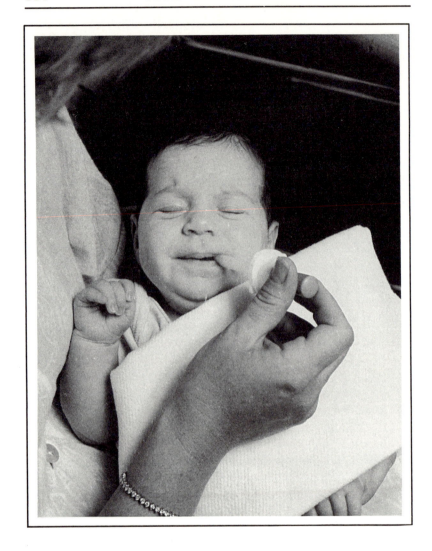

EMERGENCY TECHNIQUES

RESCUE BREATHING

Would you know what to do if your baby stopped breathing? Even though the chances are overwhelmingly against this ever happening, it is a frightening thought—but there is something you can do. Every parent should take an American Red Cross course in cardio-pulmonary resuscitation (CPR). This teaches what to do if a child stops breathing and/or the heart stops beating. The course isn't expensive, doesn't take a lot of time, and your local chapter can tell you where the nearest one is being given.

Although it's best to take the actual course so you can practice on special dolls, with a trained instructor, the following will give you an idea of the part of the technique called rescue breathing. This involves blowing air into the baby's lungs, so the brain will get the necessary oxygen until help arrives. It's called the "kiss of life." (Note: It will only work if the airway is clear, so if you suspect your baby has choked on some object, you must first remove the object.) (See CHOKING.)

1. Ask someone to dial 911 or the operator. If you are alone, begin rescue breathing, then stop briefly to call.
2. To open the baby's air passage, place one hand under the neck and gently lift. At the same time, push with the other hand on the child's forehead, tipping the head back slightly. This moves the tongue away from the back of the throat. Don't tilt too far or the airway will close.

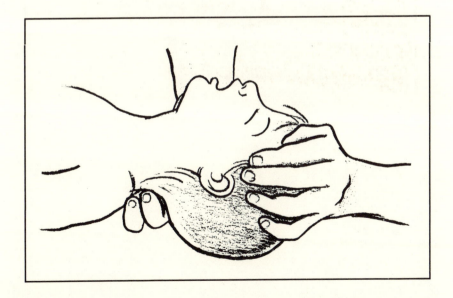

3. Check for breathing. Place your ear close to the baby's mouth and nose. Spend about five seconds looking for the chest to rise and fall while listening for the return of air.

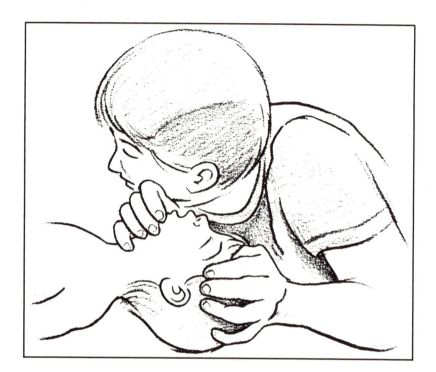

4. Maintaining the head tilt, open your mouth wide, take a breath and seal your mouth over the baby's nose and mouth.

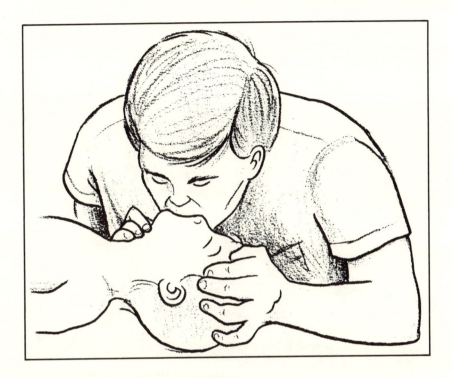

5. Blow in two slow gentle puffs of air, each puff about the amount you can hold in your cheeks, as if you were blowing out a candle. Don't give large breaths; they can damage the baby's small lungs. The baby's chest should rise.

6.   Check for a pulse on the inside of the arm, between the armpit and elbow. At the same time, look, listen and feel for breathing.

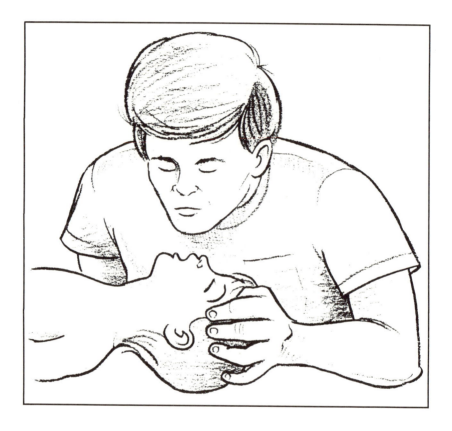

7.   If there is none, give one slow puff. Check again for pulse and breathing. Continue this cycle, giving one puff every three seconds until your baby begins breathing again or help arrives.

8.   Do not continue once the baby is breathing, or try to practice the technique on your baby.

CHOKING

It is unlikely for a very young infant to choke on a foreign object since he doesn't yet have the knack of hand-to-mouth coordination . . . but it can happen. One well-meaning toddler was discovered offering his new brother one of his favorite foods . . . a pickle! So be sure you explain to any older siblings that new babies can only drink. Also, if you give your baby a pacifier, it should be molded in one piece.

If your baby does choke on something and cannot breathe or cry, you must act quickly to remove the obstruction. Unless you can see the object, don't try to remove it with your finger—you might just push it in further. Here are the American Red Cross recommendations to relieve choking in a child under one year of age:

1. Hold the infant face down across your lap, with the head downward, supporting the head and neck. Give four quick firm blows between the shoulder blades.

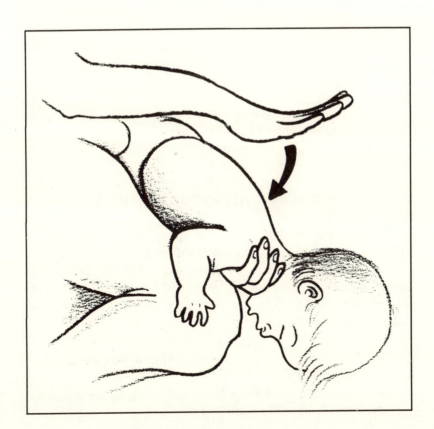

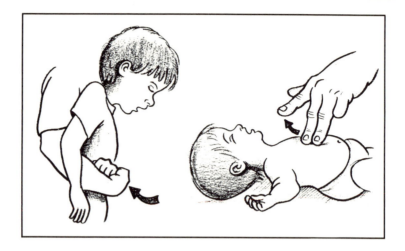

2. If the object isn't expelled, turn the infant over on a firm surface and give four quick thrusts in the middle of the chest, a finger's width below the infant's nipples.

3. Continue the combination of back blows and chest thrusts until the object is expelled or the infant becomes unconscious.

After using this technique, you should always have your baby checked by the doctor to make sure there is no damage to bones or internal organs.

YOUR EMERGENCY INFORMATION LIST

Finally, you must keep a list of emergency numbers and information by a telephone. If you don't already have one (you should, even if you don't yet have children), get it together before you expect to leave for the hospital. Those first few days at home with the new baby will be busy and you may forget about it. Here are the numbers to include on the list:

- Any Emergency: (it's usually 911, but in some areas, it may be 0 for operator)
- Paramedics or ambulance
- Nearest hospital (with address)

- Your baby's doctor
- Pharmacy (with hours and address)
- Nearest all-night pharmacy (with address)

And, since someone other than you may be making the call, also include:

- Your telephone number
- Your address
- The nearest main cross streets

QUICK REFERENCE LIST—WHEN TO CALL THE DOCTOR

- THE FONTANEL (the soft spot) IS TENSE OR BULGING.
- THE BABY HAS TURNED BLUE.
- THE BABY'S SKIN COLOR HAS BECOME YELLOWISH.
- THE BABY IS LIMP, DIFFICULT TO AROUSE OR LISTLESS.
- THE BABY HAS HAD A CONVULSION.
- YOUR BABY REFUSES TO EAT THROUGH TWO OR MORE FEEDINGS.
- YOUR BABY HAS HAD WATERY DIARRHEA THREE OR FOUR TIMES IN A ROW AND SHOWS SIGNS OF DEHYDRATION.
- THERE IS A LARGE AMOUNT OF BLOOD IN THE STOOL OR THE COLOR OF THE STOOL CHANGES TO BLACK.
- THERE IS GREEN VOMIT OR PROJECTILE VOMIT-ING (IT SHOOTS INTO THE AIR).
- THE BABY FAILS TO URINATE FOR SEVERAL HOURS OR THERE IS BLOODY URINE.
- THE BABY IS HAVING DIFFICULTY BREATHING.
- THE BABY HAS A FEVER OVER 101 DEGREES.
- YOUR BABY JUST DOESN'T LOOK OR ACT RIGHT.

CHAPTER 9
BATHING YOUR BABY

NOW, FOR THOSE MEMBERS of the family who draw the line at changing diapers, here's where they can get in on the fun part of taking care of the baby. An extra pair of hands is always helpful at bathtime. The only one who may not enjoy the event is your baby! Baths, like everything else, are a matter of individual taste. Some babies love them immediately, but most newborns scream as if they were being immersed in ice cubes instead of nice warm water, inducing instant guilt in anxious parents.

> JOAN: **None of our babies was fond of water at first and it used to upset me that they were so upset. I thought a bath should be a lovely relaxing experience**

**and I managed to blame myself—I mistakenly thought
it was my clumsiness and nervousness that was making
the baby feel insecure. Now, by the third time around,
I've realized it's just the baby's instinctive reaction.**

Fortunately, there is no need to give your baby a daily tub
bath—every two or three days is sufficient, regardless of what
grandmothers might say. Many doctors advise holding off until the
navel and circumcision wound (if done) have healed, which usually
takes up to two weeks. During this time, a sponge bath every day
or two will be more than adequate, and it gives reluctant bathers
(and nervous parents) the chance to get accustomed to the process.
Actually, there is no reason sponge baths can't be given until the
time your baby decides he's ready for the real thing.

In this chapter, you'll learn everything you need to know to
make sponge baths and tub baths easy and enjoyable for both you
and your baby! But first, to make it a safe bath—TURN DOWN
THE TEMPERATURE OF YOUR HOT WATER HEATER TO
120 DEGREES! (If you live in an apartment, you may not be able
to, so be extra careful.) That way your baby won't be scalded in
case the hot water gets turned on accidentally. In fact, you should
keep the temperature lowered all through the toddler and preschool
years, until your child is old enough to understand that the "H"
on the faucet also means "Hurt."

THE SPONGE BATH

The most comfortable way to give a sponge bath is sitting
down, so your baby can be securely cradled in your lap. The room
temperature should be comfortably warm and draft-free, but even
so, it's normal for your baby's hands and feet to turn slightly bluish.
Don't worry! Before you begin, make sure you have everything
within reach and ready to use (take the tops off). Here are the basic
items you'll need:

- flannel waterproof sheet or plastic (large enough to cover
  your lap)
- large towel
- washcloth
- cotton balls

- cotton swabs
- 2 bowls of warm water
- petroleum jelly or banana (you'll see!)
- bland soap (not deodorant, preferably unscented)
- tearless shampoo (or dandruff shampoo for cradle cap)
- fresh clothes and diaper

1.   Remove the baby's diaper on the changing table and clean off any stool. Remember to have a diaper handy in case she urinates.

2.   Place her on a large towel, with the waterproof sheet underneath the towel. Pick up the whole package and sit down. Or get ready and then have someone hand you the baby.

3.   Undress the baby . . . slowly! Most newborns instinctively hate the feel of air on their exposed skin not because of the change in temperature, but because they fear the loss of covering. So as you get down to the last layer, wrap the towel over her chest and stomach.

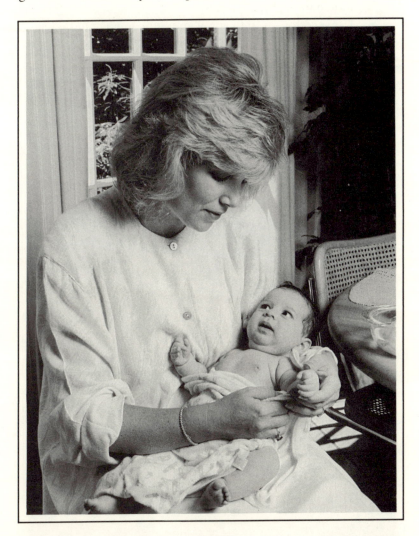

4.   Start with the body, since face washing or shampooing is more likely to produce a protest! Uncovering one area at a time, wipe the skin using fresh cotton balls moistened in one bowl of water. Then dip a washcloth in the second bowl, wring out the excess water and rinse the area well. Pat dry and cover with the towel!

- You don't have to scrub! Just soften any dried material with water until it comes off easily.
- If you use soap (not really necessary, and no more than once or twice a week to prevent drying), be sure to rinse it off thoroughly.
- Use a cotton swab to apply antiseptic to an unhealed navel or circumcision wound, if doctor advises.

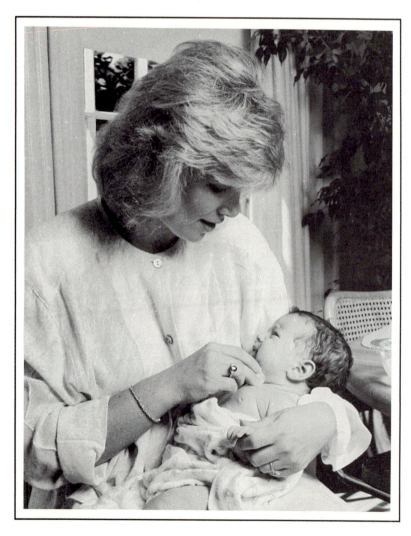

- Remember, if your son is uncircumcised, DO NOT TRY
  TO PULL BACK THE FORESKIN so you can clean under
  it. It isn't necessary and it can produce tearing, then scar
  tissue which may prevent the normal separation of the foreskin from the glans.
5. Now you're ready for the face!
   - Wipe each eye with a fresh cotton ball barely dampened in
     clean water. Wipe from the inside corner of the eye toward
     the outside.
   - Use other cotton balls, or a washcloth, and clean water to

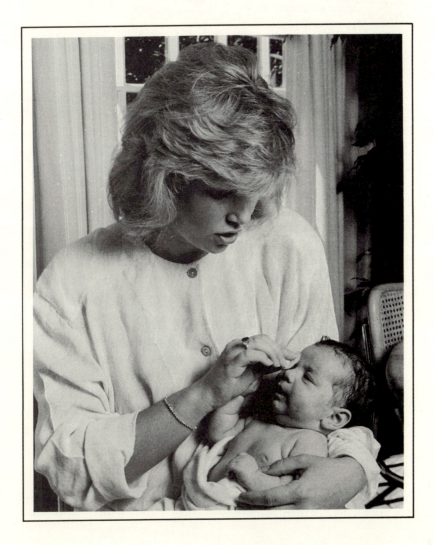

wipe off the rest of the face. (Don't forget to clean behind the ears.)

- You can use a damp cotton swab to clean the creases in the outside of the ear and the outside of the nose, but don't poke inside! The rule is . . . DON'T WASH ANYTHING YOU CAN'T SEE!

6. Finally comes the shampoo . . . which doesn't have to be traumatic! Support the baby's head with your hand and tilt her head slightly backwards. Squeeze a little clean water from the washcloth onto the scalp, and wipe it off.

- Don't be afraid to wash the "soft spot." You won't hurt the baby's brain.
- You don't need to use soap or shampoo every day—once or twice a week is fine. When you do use it, rub a little petroleum jelly (or a banana) over the baby's eyebrows. This helps prevent soap from getting into her eyes. Just remember to wipe it off!
- If your baby has cradle cap (yellowish scales on the scalp), use a dandruff shampoo daily.
- Be sure to rinse off any soap or shampoo thoroughly. It's easiest to hold the baby's head over the bowl (or sink).

Now, just pat her head dry and you're finished. (See POWDERS AND LOTIONS.) Don't be surprised if she nods off to sleep after she's diapered and dressed. Even a sponge bath is a major event for a newborn. But by taking it slow and easy in the first couple weeks, she'll get used to the idea of water and will be ready to enjoy a relaxing tub bath.

> JOAN: **I've learned to try to stay relaxed and make these first baths as soothing as possible, even if the baby is screaming her head off. I just look her in the eye and smile and I even sing a little, as if I'm having a wonderful time. Even if it doesn't always help the baby, it makes me feel better! And eventually the baby does pick up on idea that baths can be fun.**

THE TUB BATH

There are a variety of little plastic tubs that make it easier to give your baby her bath. Some have reclining seats with foam inserts to keep the baby from slipping. Actually, your kitchen sink is a really convenient spot for a bath, just place a towel or piece of foam on the bottom to prevent slipping. Some parents put a baby tub in the sink, if it fits. The important thing from your point of view is to be able to conduct the bath at a comfortable height. If you have to bend over, your back will start to protest. That's why your bathtub isn't recommended. Also, it's too soon to use the little seats with the suction cups. Wait until your baby is able to sit up.

1. THE FIRST AND MOST IMPORTANT RULE IN GIVING YOUR BABY A TUB BATH IS—NEVER LEAVE YOUR BABY ALONE IN THE TUB! It only takes seconds for a baby to slip under and drown in just a few inches of water—without making a sound! Don't answer the phone (take it off the hook or turn the ringer off so you won't be tempted). You must also have everything you need within reach, with the tops off. Basically it's the same list as for the sponge bath, except that you won't need the waterproof sheet or the bowls of water.

> JOAN: **Another thing you might find handy for the tub bath is a pair of cotton gloves! Every nervous new parent worries that the baby is "so slippery"! Well, wet babies *are* slippery and they are the first ones to sense it, probably part of the reason they're a little leary of those first baths. You can help alleviate everyone's fears by wearing cotton gloves during the bath. They really give you a better grip and they're a great way to apply soap!**

2. Now you're ready to fill the tub, but remember that it's not going to be a swimming lesson. You only need a few inches of water, no higher than the baby's nipples. It's usually best to use very little water in the first baths and gradually increase the amount.
- Always test the water temperature with your elbow or inside of your wrist, not your hands. It should feel comfortably warm, not hot, because a baby's skin is much more sensitive than yours.

3. Undress your baby, but for the first few times, don't immediately immerse her in the water. The idea is for her to get used to things gradually. Instead, wrap her in a towel and start by cleaning her face and scalp. Use the same method as for the sponge bath.

4. Then, unwrap her and gently place her in the tub holding her firmly. SUPPORT is the secret to reassuring her that baths really can be fun.

- If you're right-handed, reach your left hand around her back and hold her outside shoulder. (If you're left-handed, use your right hand.) Her head will be resting on your forearm and her body is close to yours.

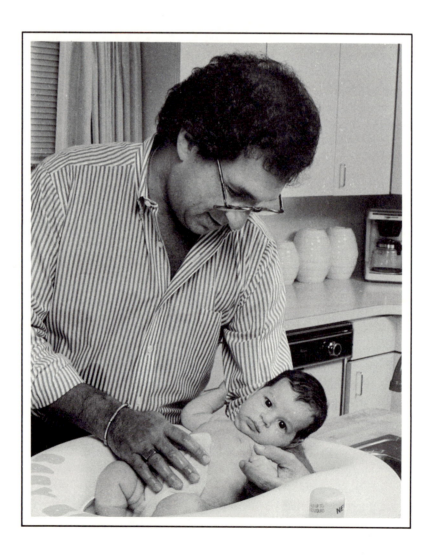

- Support her bottom with your other hand as you lower her into the water. Use this hand for bathing her while you still support her back and head.

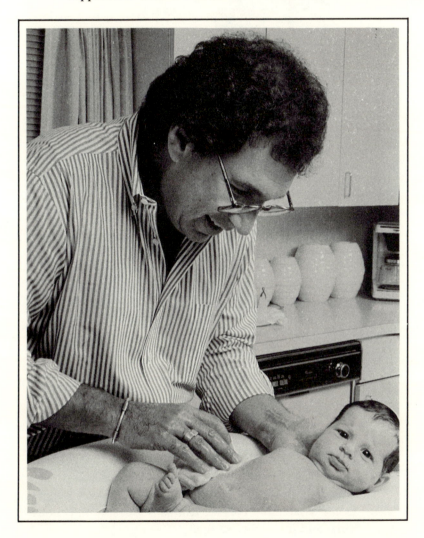

5. The washing and rinsing process is the same as for a sponge bath, but use the washcloth instead of the cotton balls. To wash her back, just lean her across your washing arm—don't turn her over.

- You don't have to use soap or shampoo every day, and then use only a little. It should be all rinsed off to prevent drying

and rashes. By the way, if your baby still develops an all-over rash, try changing the brand of soap and/or shampoo. Don't use bubble bath. It can cause urinary infections in girls, and it's highly scented.

- Remember, if your son is uncircumcised, you must not try to retract the foreskin. Clean only the outside area of the penis.

6. When she's squeaky clean, just lift her out and wrap her in a waiting towel. Make sure you dry her off thoroughly, including all the creases.

That's all there is to giving a tub bath. If your baby is enjoying the water, leave her in a little longer and make it into a playtime. Of course, if she's still frightened, get it over with quickly and go back to sponge baths for a few days. Sooner or later, almost all babies come to love their baths.

Oh, and one more bit of advice for whoever's doing the bathing—wear an apron, preferably waterproof. You're bound to get splashed and dripped on!

POWDERS AND LOTIONS

Many parents feel they have to finish off a bath by covering the baby with powder and/or lotion. In fact, a baby's skin has natural oils, so there's no reason to rub in a moisturizing lotion unless the skin seems unusually dry. Remember, it's normal for a newborn's skin to peel during the first week or so.

There's also no need to routinely cover your baby with powder, which tends to collect in the creases and can cause a rash. If she has a heat rash or case of baby acne, a little cornstarch (but not around the diaper area) might be helpful. If you use a baby powder, it should have a cornstarch base, not talc. But don't just sprinkle it on—your baby might breathe some in. Instead, shake a little in your hand and then smooth it on the rash.

Actually, using a scented baby powder or lotion is really a case of "gilding the lily." Babies, especially when they're freshly bathed, have their own delicious smell. Take a good sniff—it's irresistible!

CHAPTER 10
YOUR BABY'S CRYING

CRYING IS ONE OF the most difficult things for new parents to deal with and it's understandable—nobody wants to see their precious little baby unhappy. But it helps to understand that crying is simply an instinctive survival technique for newborns.

> JOAN: **That's why it's so important to follow your natural instincts to go to your baby whenever she cries. You may hear lots of advice from friends or older relatives like, "If you pick her up every time she cries, you'll just spoil her" or "It's good for a baby to cry; it exercises the lungs." Don't believe it! Babies don't cry to exercise their lungs.**
>
> **As for spoiling, modern medical opinion is best expressed by pediatrician and newborn behavior ex-**

pert, Dr. T. Berry Brazelton who believes "You can never spoil a baby with too much love and attention. Your baby is helpless, and when she needs you, she communicates in the only way she can, by crying. You teach her trust and security with lots of loving attention."

Here are some of the things your baby is communicating through her crying. As you respond to her you'll soon learn to recognize the different messages.

THE REASONS FOR CRYING

Hunger.

Hunger is, of course, the most common reason that newborns cry. Every two to three hours, your baby will start to wake up with a few complaining whimpers. Then if he's not picked up and fed, his cries will become louder, more insistent and rhythmic. If you're not sure, just try letting him suck on your finger or a pacifier. A hungry baby will let you know (usually in less than a minute) that he wants the real thing.

Sucking Needs and Pacifiers.

All babies have a need to suck, they even do it in the womb; however, some have more of a need than can be satisfied during feedings. If you're nursing and your baby likes to "hang out" on the breast after or between feedings, she might be satisfied, but you're likely to have sore nipples.

What else can you do? Well, you can encourage your baby to suck on her fist or thumb, but in the first few weeks, she may not be too efficient at finding it. The alternative is giving a pacifier, an object that can provoke a barrage of criticism from well-meaning friends and relatives. The main objection seems to be that once a baby is hooked on a pacifier, it will take years to break her loose. It's more likely that the baby herself will give up a pacifier after a few months, especially if you don't make it into a habit by shoving one in every time your baby complains. Pacifiers are also criticized as being unhygienic, but it's easy enough to keep one clean with soap and water. Other people simply are bothered by the unaesthetic look of a child with a plug in her mouth.

> JOAN: **Our pediatrician, like most doctors, is not against giving the baby a pacifier, as long as it isn't used as a substitute for cuddling and physical contact. When a baby is tired or overstimulated, the sucking may also help relieve tension and soothe her. The only warning is to use a pacifier that is made in one piece so the nipple can't come off and cause choking. And, of course, YOU SHOULD NEVER TIE A PACIFIER ON A CORD AROUND THE BABY'S NECK—babies have choked to death that way!**
>
> **If you're breastfeeding, it might be best to hold off on a pacifier until your baby has mastered the art of nursing, then she won't be confused by the different sucking technique. When she's old enough to find her thumb, you may prefer to switch from the pacifier. Thumbs have the big advantage of not getting lost in the middle of the night!**

Thirst.

Newborns usually get enough liquid in their usual feedings of breast milk or formula. They don't need additional water. But if the weather is very hot or the baby has a fever, he may cry before his expected feeding time because he is thirsty. A breastfed baby can nurse a few minutes, getting the thinner foremilk that is lower in calories, and satisfy his thirst. Or, when he's developed a good nursing technique and won't be confused by a nipple, you can offer a bottle of plain water. If a baby is formula-fed, he really doesn't need the full calorie content of the formula, so a little bottle of plain boiled water (no sugar) will satisfy him.

Being Uncomfortable.

As you learned in the last chapter, newborns are likely to cry whenever they are undressed. It's the feeling of air on their bodies that makes them uncomfortable, so don't be afraid that you're being clumsy. You can help by covering his chest and tummy with a little towel until you can get him into his new clothing.

Many parents believe that babies cry when their diapers are wet or soiled, because they stop crying when they're changed. While this might be true of older babies, studies have shown that newborns don't seem to cry to get their diapers changed. It's really the act of picking the baby up and handling him that quiets the cries. Of course, fresh diapers certainly will help prevent diaper rash.

Babies also rarely cry when they're too warm; they just sweat and get prickly heat! On the other hand, it's normal for babies to cry when they are feeling cold and this is actually a self-protective reaction. The crying causes the baby's body to generate heat and he warms up.

JOAN: **During the night, when we put the baby back into the crib after a feeding, it really helps to first warm the mattress with a heating pad. That way there's no shock of a cold mattress to wake a sleepy baby, but never let a baby sleep on a heating pad.**

Illness.

Babies are also likely to cry when they are ill. This is more of a fussing, whiney cry that may be accompanied by symptoms such as fever, diarrhea or vomiting.

Pain.

Pain usually produces a different type of crying. It starts with a sudden catching of breath and then continues as a piercing scream until he is out of breath. There's a moment of silence as he takes another breath and then the wail begins again. It's a sound that's guaranteed to strike fear in a parent's heart! Sometimes a baby might hold his breath so long before letting out a scream that he momentarily turns bluish. Don't panic, it's not dangerous.

You should always check to make sure there is no external reason for the crying, such as being stuck with a diaper pin or having a thread in the foot of his sleeper wound around his toe. However, the most common source of pain, especially if it occurs within half an hour or so after a feeding, is air that's been swallowed during a feeding and is trapped in his tummy or has passed into his intestines. Pick him up and try burping him (see BURPING YOUR BABY). The air may be released from either end of the baby and this usually brings relief.

Colic.

When a baby cries a lot, seems to be in pain and is very gassy, you often hear that "he must have colic." But what exactly is "colic"? First of all, it's not an illness or a disease. And unless it happens after every feeding, it's not likely to be an adverse reaction to formula or cow's milk (see p. 11, When Something Doesn't Agree). The American Academy of Pediatrics simply defines colic as "severe abdominal discomfort in a young infant." It's really just a word that describes this specific set of "symptoms" or behavior:

- A baby who wasn't previously fussy begins crying more at around the age of two to four weeks.
- The crying follows a regular pattern, occuring every day at the same time, usually in the evening.
- The baby usually falls asleep easily, then wakes up crying intensely.
- The baby may draw his legs up, his abdomen may be bloated, and he may pass gas.
- Nothing seems to comfort him for very long, and the crying may continue for an hour or two until he goes to sleep.
- Other than this one period of the day, the baby seems content.

No one is really sure why some babies (fortunately it isn't as common as is thought) show these signs of colic. One theory attributes it to excessive swallowing of air during feeding, but doctors point out it would then occur after every meal, instead of only during one period of the day. The same logic rules out an allergy to cow's milk. However, if a mother is breastfeeding and tends to eat a particular food at the same time every day, the baby might be reacting to that food. It may be that crying (for any reason) results in air being swallowed which then causes a cycle of pain and more crying. Other theories blame it on the baby's immature neurological or digestive system. The good news is that whatever causes colic to appear, it usually disappears by the time a baby is three months old. You often hear it called "three month colic."

Once your doctor has eliminated any other reasons for the crying episodes, such as illness or a reaction to food, and you're fairly sure you really do have a colicky baby, what can you do? You can try the various methods of soothing a fussy baby, such as music, rocking, giving a pacifier or swaddling (see p. 141, HOW TO SWADDLE). Warming the crib with a heating pad and laying the baby on his tummy also may soothe him. If the colic is severe, your doctor may prescribe medication; however, you should NEVER give medicine or a sedative without consulting your doctor.

But, remember, sometimes nothing helps and even the most confident, competent and patient of parents can become frustrated and upset when they can't stop their baby from crying. If you're one of them, you must recognize that it's NOT YOUR FAULT. You must stop feeling guilty. Don't be afraid to discuss your feelings with your doctor so he can reassure you that your baby isn't crying because of something you did or didn't do.

Loneliness and Fussiness.

Newborns also fuss and cry because they need the comfort of being held. For nine months the only environment the baby knows is soft, quiet and always the same temperature, where she is gently rocked and can hear the soothing rhythmic sound of a heartbeat. The closest adults can come is swaying in a hammock on a warm beach, listening to the waves—guaranteed to put anyone to sleep. Then suddenly your baby is apart from you, by herself, lying on a hard surface. It's only natural for her to feel lonely.

JOAN: **The solution is obvious and easy: just pick your baby up and cuddle her until she feels comfortable again. After all, in "primitive" societies where everyone worked, it was necessary for babies to spend a lot of time being carried by the mother or another member of the family.**

But you may worry: "Will the baby be spoiled if she's picked up too much?" The answer from doctors and child psychologists is "NO!" You must remember that a newborn baby just doesn't consciously think, "If I cry I'll be picked up." She's not trying to manipulate you, she's just expressing an instinctive need for closeness. When you respond to that need, you are teaching her that the world is a comfortable place that she can trust and feel secure in.

It's not surprising a recent study has shown it's important to pick your baby up even when she's NOT crying. By six weeks of age, those babies in the study who had been carried around or cuddled an extra hour or two a day (when they weren't crying) actually cried and fussed less. This was especially noticeable during

the four P.M. to midnight "fuss period," when crankiness was cut in half!

Manufacturers have been responding to this new/old need to carry a baby close to you by making baby carriers that allow you to "wear" your baby while you do other things. You can also improvise a sling using a crib sheet or a receiving blanket. And this is one way that fathers can really get involved during these first weeks.

HOW TO SWADDLE

When you can't hold your baby, or when she is sleeping, you can help satisfy her need for physical contact by swaddling her. In the past, swaddling was used in the belief it would help keep the baby's back straight. When that was shown to be just an "old wives' tale," the art of swaddling fell into disuse. Now, doctors recommend swaddling as a method of soothing newborns, but many new parents are a little hazy about the proper way to do it.

JOAN: I sure was and this was one time Dr. Brown couldn't help. He said, "Something always sticks out whenever I try it." But a baby nurse taught me this basic technique to securely swaddle a baby. It's easy and it usually works!

1. Receiving blankets are very convenient, but if the weather is very hot, use any light gauzy material for wrapping. Just be sure it's washable!
2. Spread out the blanket and lay your baby on her back in the middle, with her limbs in their normal position and her head over the edge. Don't try to straighten her arms or legs.
3. Bring one top corner of the blanket diagonally across her shoulder and tuck it firmly under her knees. Be sure that her hands are in a position where she can suck on them if she wants to. Some babies prefer to have their arms free. In that case, just bring the blanket under the arm and across her body.

4. You can fold the bottom of the blanket up over the legs, or if it's long, just leave it down.

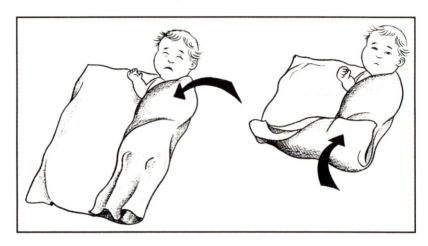

5. Take the other side of the blanket and fold it firmly over her body and legs.
6. Then tuck it under her body. Her weight will keep it secure whether she lies on her tummy, back or side.

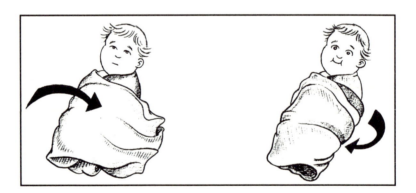

The trick is to wrap her tightly enough so that she doesn't move inside the blanket, which should move as she moves. (Of course, it shouldn't be so tight that it cuts off circulation!) You may worry that swaddling is restricting her and makes her feel "trapped." Actually, this firm wrapping makes her feel secure. She'll let you know by kicking and struggling when it's time to unwrap her.

CHAPTER 11
YOUR BABY'S SLEEP

UNTIL YOU SETTLE INTO a routine, those first few days after you bring your baby home from the hospital may seem like a busy blur with all the frequent feedings, and the frequent diaper changing, and the bathing. However, newborns have one big advantage— many of them really do sleep a lot! In this chapter you'll learn everything you need to know about your baby's sleep.

Sleep Patterns.

Exactly how much time do newborns spend sleeping? According to Dr. Richard Ferber, Director of the Center for Pediatric Sleep Disorders at Children's Hospital in Boston, the typical one-week-old baby sleeps a total of sixteen half-hours out of every twenty-four hours. By the time he's one month old, he still sleeps an average of fifteen half-hours. Unfortunately, at the beginning, he's likely to wake up every two to three hours for a feeding, or even more often if he's breastfed.

Sleep patterns actually start developing before birth. At six or seven months, REM (the more active type of sleep) appears, then by eight months, the fetus also has periods of non-REM ("Quiet Sleep"). When newborns first fall asleep, they go into the REM stage in which the higher centers of the brain receive stimulation from the deeper, more primitive areas. This may be sensory input that is important to the development of the brain's higher centers. No one knows if infants dream, but in REM sleep your baby may twitch, his eyes will move under his closed eyelids and he may even smile. Don't worry that your newborn seems to be a "light sleeper." It's not until three months or so that babies immediately go into the deep non-REM type of sleep when they're "out like a light." It's also encouraging that research shows even if your baby isn't a "good sleeper" during those first few days in the hospital it's not an indication of things to come!

Once your baby is home, he will usually start developing a pattern of sleep and wake periods at around two weeks, gradually sleeping longer stretches at night. If he seems to be settling into a longer sleep during the day and he's up more at night, you can help change this pattern by waking him earlier and earlier from the long daytime sleep period unless you both are also night owls! Most babies naturally put themselves on a regular twenty-four-hour schedule, but it may take as long as ten weeks to develop.

JOAN: **Now for the big question that looms larger and larger for weary parents, especially breastfeeding mothers. "When will the baby start sleeping through the night?" The answer is most full-term healthy babies will sleep through the night by the time they are three or four months old, but a few may take as long as six months. So if some mother proudly brags that her baby slept through by two weeks, simply grit your teeth and reply, "Lucky you."**

Just don't worry that it's your fault your baby is still getting up, or feel there's something you can do to rush things along, like letting him cry! Dr. Ferber does recommend this as part of his method of treating

problem sleepers, but only for babies who are at least six months old. In these first few months, most babies need at least one feeding during the night. Of course, once breastfeeding was well-established, I had no qualms about Michael getting up to give the baby a bottle when I felt I really needed some uninterrupted sleep.

As for the suggestion that giving solid food will help keep a baby from getting hungry in the middle of the night, that's just another "old wives' tale." Remember, the doctors say your baby's digestive system isn't ready for solids until he's at least four months old!

Where to Sleep.

Whether you have a full-size crib, a bassinet, a cradle or a dresser drawer, your newborn will sleep just fine. Keep in mind the advice in Chapter 3 . . . PREPARING THE NEST.

- The mattress should be firm, so the baby can easily move his head to find breathing space. Don't use a pillow as a mattress.
- Don't put in a pillow or large stuffed animals.
- Regularly check the frame of the crib or bassinet to make sure the fittings are tight and it won't collapse.

JOAN: **And, since the mattress is probably covered in plastic, it's a good idea to place a square of rubber sheeting, a diaper or even a terrycloth towel between the crib sheet and the mattress. Plastic isn't absorbent and if the baby spits up or perspires, it could make him uncomfortable enough to wake up. Newborns also feel more secure and soothed by contact with a softer surface. If the room temperature is cool, you might even prewarm the mattress a little with a heating pad, but NEVER allow the baby to sleep on it.**

About whether or not to bring the baby into your own bed to sleep, that's really a matter of personal preference. In the past, many doctors advised against it for psychological reasons. By the way, they are not concerned a parent may roll over onto the baby and suffocate him. Doctors point out that even newborns can protest loudly enough to rouse a sleeping parent. However, the consensus now is that there's no harm in keeping a baby in the parents' bed as long as BOTH parents are in favor of it. This practice is really the norm in non-Western cultures and it certainly has the advantage that no one has to get up during the night to get the baby for a feeding! On the down side, babies aren't quiet sleepers, so you may be awakened more often.

Sleeping Positions.

What position should a baby sleep in? This question can result in some heated arguments, especially if a grandmother grew up in Europe where infants usually sleep on their backs. The feeling there is that a baby can suffocate if he sleeps on his tummy. But in America, infants are commonly placed on their tummies. Many parents are afraid that if a baby sleeps on his back, he can choke if he spits up or vomits. The truth is, these beliefs are just two more "old wives' tales." A healthy baby won't choke or suffocate whether he sleeps on his tummy, his back or his side. However, if he does tend to spit up or has colic, he may be more comfortable lying on his tummy.

Sudden Infant Death Syndrome (SIDS)

Many mothers worry needlessly about SIDS. Actually, this syndrome (also known as crib death) only affects an estimated two infants out of every one thousand born each year. It is most likely to occur during sleep, suddenly and without warning, between the second and fourth months. Experts in this area strongly emphasize that SIDS is definitely NOT a result of a baby's sleeping position, external suffocation, vomiting or choking. In fact, SIDS cannot be predicted or prevented, it doesn't happen because of anything parents or care givers did or did not do.

Unfortunately, no one yet knows what does cause SIDS. Some researchers believe these babies may have had subtle heart or breathing problems since birth, perhaps due to immature development in a part of the brain. Infants are at slightly higher risk if they were born prematurely, had a low birth weight, or had a brother or sister who died of SIDS.

If you suspect your baby may have had an episode where he briefly stopped breathing, called sleep apnea, after which his skin color was bluish or pale, bring it to the attention of your doctor. It may be a symptom of a treatable condition or it may indicate the baby is at higher risk of SIDS. A high-risk baby can be hooked up to a home monitor that sounds an alarm if breathing stops.

Pets and Your Baby

In the past, dogs and cats were often unfairly blamed for causing crib death. People believed the pet had climbed into the crib and suffocated the baby. Now experts know that SIDS is not caused by any kind of external suffocation. But is it a good idea to allow a pet into the baby's room?

> JOAN: **Since we now have a cat, this was something new to worry about after Sarah was born. Dr. Brown reassured us the cat would not suffocate the baby, but he also pointed out it's not a good idea to mix newborns and pets for health reasons. Dogs and cats may cause allergies and they may carry infections, so he advised keeping our cat out of the baby's room. Dogs have also been known to become jealous and attack babies. NEVER LEAVE A BABY OR SMALL CHILD ALONE WITH A DOG.**

Helping Your Baby to Go to Sleep . . . and Stay Asleep.

Here's another bit of unfounded advice: "Be quiet, or you'll wake the baby!" Well, you don't have to go around whispering because babies don't need quiet, or even darkness, in order to sleep. Just think of how often you've seen a baby soundly sleeping on a bus or in a department store. Of course, a toddler's screams or loud music may startle him, but normal room noise and conversation is fine. In fact, if a baby does get accustomed to sleeping in a dark quiet room, he may have difficulty going to sleep in any other

Some babies drift easily off to sleep and others need a little more help settling down. Take note of the word "help" and keep in mind there is nothing anyone can do to "make" a baby go to sleep! However, there is a large variety of techniques and tricks that may help a fussy, overtired or overstimulated baby settle into dreamland. You may have to experiment a bit to find out which method is the most soothing. Each newborn is an individual and what works like a charm for one may just irritate another baby.

A few of these methods were discussed in the last chapter, YOUR BABY'S CRYING, but here's a fairly comprehensive list compiled from doctors and parents (the real experts):

- PACIFIER, THUMB or FIST. This will satisfy any need to suck and it may relieve tension. If a sleeping baby is disturbed, sucking often keeps him from completely waking up.
- SWADDLING. Many newborns feel more secure when they are firmly wrapped and their jerky movements are less likely to disturb their sleep. (See p. 141, HOW TO SWADDLE.)
- PHYSICAL CONTACT. Newborns are also comforted by being close to your body, so try cuddling your baby or "wearing" him in a sling or carrier.
- ROCKING. This is a very effective way to relax a baby. If it doesn't work, you may be rocking too slowly. Research has shown the best rate is around sixty rocks a minute or one every second. While you can rock your baby in his carriage or cradle, the most relaxing place for you is a good old-fashioned rocking chair!
- WALKING. If you'd rather get some exercise, go for walk either inside the house or out . . . with the baby, of course.
- RHYTHMICAL or MONOTONOUS SOUNDS. These seem to work by blocking out whatever internal stimuli are disturbing the baby. Try soft music or a recording of a heartbeat—something newborns recognize easily. Also ef-

fective: the sound of a fan, an engine or a vacuum cleaner (you don't actually have to do the vacuuming unless your house needs it). Just be sure the music or sound doesn't stop before the baby is completely asleep or the change may rouse him again.

- DRIVING. Babies love to sleep in a moving car, but the problem is to keep moving, otherwise they wake up. If you go for a drive, try to pick a highway with no stoplights and have exact change ready for any toll booths. There are also gadgets you can attach to a crib which simulate both the motion and the sound of a moving car. You'll more than pay for one with the money you save on gas.

And don't forget, anyone can get in on the act of soothing a baby to sleep and this is one activity most mothers will be more than happy to hand over. I figured out this "football hold" for Jamie that always put her out cold and it's worked with Lindsay and our new baby Sarah. Just give a little jiggle or swing now and then and don't worry about any comments from the older generation on how that's no way to handle a little baby. By the way, our pediatrician approves!

EPILOGUE
. . . AND THEN COME THE "BABY BLUES"

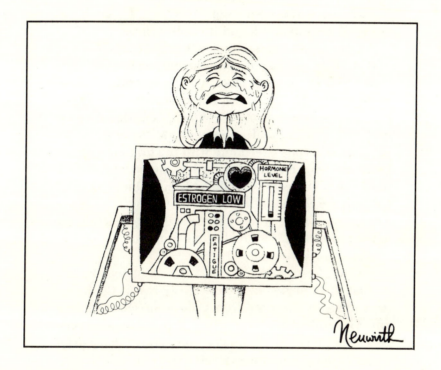

JOAN: Now that you've learned everything you need to know about your newborn baby, I'd like you to take some time out for yourself. After the baby is born, you experience so many new feelings, some of them terrific and some that are not so great. Just as with everything else, it helps a lot if you understand what's happening to you.

In the first place, you're probably pretty exhausted, especially if you're breastfeeding and you're up every two or three hours. Well, do yourself a favor and sleep whenever your baby sleeps, or at least lie down, close your eyes and rest. I know this is easier to say than do, at least for me. With the first babies, I'd be up during the night, then when it was daytime, I felt I should be doing normal daytime things like writing thank you notes, calling people and having them over to see the baby. You can quickly become a basket case if you keep it up. This time, I tried to be better at resting and found it really helped.

One reason it's so important to get enough rest is that it helps you handle postpartum depression, also called PPD or the term I like, "the baby blues." Some of the symptoms are sudden tears, irrational fears concerning the baby's health, feelings of inadequacy as a mother and wife, and an inability to make even the simplest decisions. Certainly with the first baby, I got home and was hit with this heavy emotional feeling I just couldn't explain. I would let feelings build up until I'd pick the closest, littlest, stupidest thing as a reason to blow up. Then when I realized I was reacting all out of proportion, I would begin to question my sanity. Now I know better.

Don't let anyone tell you, "It's all in your head" or that it's a sign you unconsciously resent the baby. According to the American College of Obstetricians and Gynecologists, postpartum depression is a very real physical reaction caused by the sudden sharp drop in your estrogen hormone levels that were so high during pregnancy. Although it doesn't affect all women to the same degree, the chances are about fifty-fifty you will experience some of these feelings.

What can you do about it? Well, to begin with, just knowing this is a common experience among new mothers, the reasons behind it and the fact that it is temporary will help a lot. Remember, information relieves anxiety. So be sure and discuss PPD with your obstetrician BEFORE you deliver so you know what to expect. I wish that doctors would also meet with every prospective father and explain the physical reasons for PPD and what to expect. It really helps if your husband is sympathetic and understanding of what seems like your strange behavior. But even so, it's tough for someone else to know what you are going through.

Unfortunately, most of us aren't good at expressing our feelings and things can quickly build up. I've learned it's so important to sit down and say "You know, I've got to tell you something, I'm really feeling terrible, like crying all the time." Your husband's uncritical support can go a long way to getting you through this period. However, if the depression continues or you feel yourself out of control, you should talk to your doctor as soon as possible. Severe cases of PPD may be alleviated by taking the hormone progesterone, which your doctor may want to prescribe.

Finally, I'd like to pass along some hard-earned advice to any new mother who plans to go back to work. "Don't be in too much of a rush!" I think we've all gotten too caught up in the idea that "you can do it all," and I worry about having been a role model and setting up unfair expectations. My job has unique advantages. I have incredible flexibility and I was able to take my babies to work with me, so the first time I went back to work at five weeks and the second time at three weeks! Even in this ideal situation, it was too soon. You're physically still recuperating, you tire easily and you probably haven't lost—nor should you expect to—all the weight you gained. So you don't look or feel your best which makes it even more difficult to get back into the swing of things, no matter what your job.

This time I stayed home a full eight weeks with the baby and I highly recommend it if at all possible. If you have a limited amount of maternity leave, it's better to work right up to delivery and take all the time you can after the baby's born. These first weeks are so very special. . . .

APPENDIX

For more information, contact the following organizations:

AMERICAN ACADEMY OF ALLERGY AND IMMUNOLOGY
611 East Wells Street
Milwaukee, WI 53202
(414) 272-6701

AMERICAN ACADEMY OF PEDIATRICS
141 Northwest Point Road
P.O. Box 927
Elk Grove Village, IL 60007
(312) 228-5005

AMERICAN COLLEGE OF ALLERGISTS
800 East Northwest Highway
Suite 101
Mount Prospect, IL 60056
(312) 255-0380

AMERICAN COLLEGE OF OBSTETRICIANS AND GYNECOLOGISTS
600 Maryland Avenue, S.W.
Washington, DC 20024
(202) 638-5577 (Resource Center)

AMERICAN LUNG ASSOCIATION
1740 Broadway
New York, NY 10019
(212) 315-8700

AMERICAN RED CROSS
431 18th Street, N.W.
Washington, DC 20006
(202) 737-8300

ASTHMA & ALLERGY FOUNDATION OF AMERICA
1302 18th Street, N.W.
Suite 303
Washington, DC 20036
(202) 293-2950

CENTER FOR SCIENCE IN THE PUBLIC INTEREST (CSPI)
1501 16th Street, N.W.
Washington, DC 20036
(202) 332-9110

CENTERS FOR DISEASE CONTROL
1600 Clifton Road
Atlanta, GA 30333
(404) 329-3311

FOOD AND DRUG ADMINISTRATION
5600 Fishers Lane
Rockville, MD 20857
(202) 443-1544

LA LECHE LEAGUE
P.O. Box 1209
9616 Minneapolis Avenue
Franklin Park, IL 60131-8209
(312) 455-7730 (HOT LINE)

MARCH OF DIMES BIRTH DEFECTS FOUNDATION
1275 Mamaroneck Avenue
White Plains, NY 10605
(914) 428-7100

NATIONAL CENTER FOR THE PREVENTION OF SIDS
(800) 638-7437 (except Md.)

NATIONAL COMMITTEE FOR PREVENTION OF CHILD ABUSE
332 South Michigan Avenue
Suite 950
Chicago, IL 60604
(312) 663-3520

NATIONAL INSTITUTES OF HEALTH
9000 Rockville Pike
Bethesda, MD 20892
(202) 496-4000

NATIONAL PASSENGER SAFETY ASSOCIATION
1050 17th Street, N.W.
Suite 770
Washington, D.C. 20036
(202) 429-0515

NATIONAL SAFETY COUNCIL
1705 DeSales, N.W.
Suite 300
Washington, DC 20036
(202) 293-2270

SUDDEN INFANT DEATH SYNDROME INFORMATION CLEARINGHOUSE
3520 Prospect St., N.W.
Ground Floor, Suite 1
Washington, DC 20057
(202) 625-8410

U.S. CONSUMER PRODUCT SAFETY COMMISSION
Washington, DC 20207
(800) 638-2772 (Continental U.S.)
(800) 492-8363 (Maryland residents)
(800) 638-8333 (Alaska, Hawaii, Puerto Rico, Virgin Islands)

U.S. DEPARTMENT OF AGRICULTURE
14th & Independence Avenue, S.W.
Washington, DC 20250
(202) 447-2791